THE CHA

HOW A CENTURY OF WOMEN WERE

ROBBED OF SAFE CHILDBIRTH

John T. Queenan, MD

To my wife, Carrie, who makes every new day exciting

and

*to the mothers of the world, whose devotion, caring,
and sacrifices are the lifeline of humanity*

Acknowledgements

There are many people to thank for their editing, guidance, and encouragement in writing this book: Chuck Emig, James E. Swan, Professor Hal Cook, Samantha Kelly, Joan E. Quigley, Tom Barbash, Ralph Hale, and Audrey Wolfe.

To those who gave their technical expertise I offer my great appreciation: Rebecca D. Rinehart, Rebecca S. Benner, Mary Hyde, Debra G. Scarborough, Heidi L. Vermette, Michele Prince, Lucy Reid and the Medical History Department at the Royal College of Obstetricians and Gynaecologists, Penny Hutchens, as well as Emmanuel College at Cambridge.

I would also like to thank many friends and colleagues who encouraged me to try my hand at a modern history and helped me along the way: John Studd, Stuart Campbell, Charles Rodeck, John Bonnar, Yinka Oyelese, Keith Lindgren, Vernon Katz, Stuart Taylor, James R. Scott, Gerald Turner, Helen Dixon, Carrie Brown, Tom Melly, and Patti Morehouse. And of course, thank you to Janet and Colin Doe for maintaining the Woodham Mortimer Hall as a trust house.

I thank my children, John T. Queenan Jr. MD and Lynne Q. Beauregard, who have reviewed progressive versions of this book. And, finally, my wife Carrie Neher Queenan for her constant help, advice, and pursuit of this historical mystery. She never lost hope. I am very grateful.

Table of Contents

Preface

This is the story of a remarkable family, the Chamberlens, who conceived a simple but ingenious device that was to have an enormous impact on the mortality of women and babies in Britain, and ultimately, the world. In pre-modern times, before the advent of general anesthesia and operative delivery, the fate of a woman in childbirth depended entirely on her ability in labor to move the baby through the birth canal. When the passenger was larger than the passageway the labor became obstructed and both mother and baby died. This was the plight of women through all of human history.

But in the late-16th century, in Southampton England, Peter Chamberlen and his father William constructed an instrument to overcome this lethal problem and in so doing inaugurated a new era in medicine. They and their successors saved many lives with this device. Nevertheless, they resolved to keep their invention a family secret for five generations and thus deprived millions of women of its benefits. This story takes place in Europe long before there was any knowledge of bacterial infections and centuries before cesarean deliveries could be performed.

Peter used the secret instrument to gain fame as a male midwife and personal physician to royalty. His younger brother, also named Peter, earned a widespread reputation for working miracles with obstructed labors. Both were "mere" barber-surgeons who were forbidden to prescribe the kinds of remedies their betters, the physicians, were entitled to use. Hence they repeatedly ran afoul of the Royal College of Physicians for "illegal and evil" practices. Nevertheless, both continued to practice and prosper, and together they raised and taught their art to the son of Peter the Younger, who was also named Peter and was referred to as Dr. Peter. Dr. Peter went on to become a highly respected physician, providing his father and uncle the opportunity to live vicariously through him as respected medical men in London. Dr. Peter's three sons also became physicians and used the family invention to practice midwifery, while continuing to keep its existence secret. Unbelievably, the secret that transformed the practice of obstetrics was not revealed for one and a half centuries.

For over three decades, I have been fascinated by the story of the Chamberlens and have read widely on the subject. When I first encountered them in *The Chamberlens and the Midwifery Forceps* by Aveling (originally published in 1882), I was amazed to read this comment in the preface:

> "Nearly all writers of systematic works on Obstetrics seemed to have considered it necessary, when they arrived at the descriptions of the midwifery forceps, to give a slight sketch of the Chamberlen family. I have no hesitation in stating that all these biographical essays, including previous attempts of my own, are more or less incorrect. I could occupy pages in recording the errors made by writers of the highest reputation when dealing with this subject; it is sufficient, however, to warn the profession against accepting as true any account of the Chamberlens published before this date, no matter how trustworthy in other respects the author may be." (Aveling 1882)

Initially surprised by Aveling's bold statement, I remained skeptical until I had read many more texts on the subject. The more I read, the more it became clear to me that no one had gone to the extent that Aveling had gone to research the original documents. He had obtained permission from the Lord Bishop of London to consult the Registers of the See and the Vicar General and from the President of the Royal College of Physicians of London to view the "Annals of the Royal College." In addition, the Master of the Barber's Company, which still exists today, permitted him to make excerpts of the "Annals of the

Barber-Surgeons." I was forced to conclude that any facts beyond what Aveling was able to discover about the Chamberlens would have to remain a mystery, but an intriguing subject for speculation. In this presentation, the Chamberlens are true characters as I perceive them. In several instances I have presented scenes which history records took place but for which no written account can be uncovered. When presenting such speculative recreation, I clearly state that this is as I perceive the situation was, and block off these "recreations" with three asterisks in the middle of the page (* * *).

In creating this narrative account about a major historical medical invention, I have drawn heavily upon the authoritative work of Aveling and have quoted his work when applicable. Other vital references include Mauriceau's documentation of Hugh Chamberlen's visit to Paris, Radcliffe's excellent insight into history of the forceps, and Wilson's descriptions of the childbirth customs of the times. Finally, the Diaries of Samuel Pepys and Percival Willughby have provided invaluable insight into the events of the 1660s. A complete bibliography can be found at the end of the book

This book is offered with respect and reverence for inventive genius. It is important to share the momentous advance that the Chamberlen forceps represented in overcoming one of humanity's greatest scourges: women's death in childbirth. Similarly, it is important to see how self-promotion and avarice can prevail over good. Many situations in medicine today are not dissimilar to those in this story.

John Thomas Queenan, MD
Washington, DC, November 25, 2014

Chapter 1   William Chamberlen - 1569

Childbirth is supposed to be a creative, uplifting, and joyous event, but for Dr. William Chamberlen, a Huguenot physician practicing in 16th century England, helping a midwife in trouble with a delivery was far from his favorite thing. Actually, he dreaded this task. First, it was unheard of to have a man present in the birth chamber, so he was never welcome in the patient's home. Second, as a physician trained in Paris with skills in midwifery, William was only called as a last resort when the baby was, in most cases, already dead. Third, when called to see a woman in labor he never knew her, for she was a patient of the midwife. Finally, what he was expected to do was repugnant to him.

When a midwife summoned William to a patient's home, it was typically after two or three days of exhausting labor. The setting was solemn and desperate. The father, already resigned to the loss of his baby and possibly his wife, would feel little relief with the arrival of the physician. The mother, whose condition would have deteriorated, probably would not have even been aware that help had arrived. The midwife, however, was grateful for she knew she was in the midst of a calamity and now she had someone with whom to share the trouble.

Childbirth in the 16th and 17th century in England was a dangerous event. Fifteen mothers and 100 babies died for every 1000 deliveries (Towler 1986). Every pregnant woman knew of someone who had died in childbirth. Most births took place in homes; all were vaginal deliveries, and nearly all by midwives or female relatives who had little or no training. While most deliveries probably resulted in a healthy mother and baby, many did not. For those, there were no cesarean deliveries to get the midwives out of trouble. The mother had no other options but to deliver the baby vaginally.

The medical historian Speert describes the problems of early cesarean births. In the 17th century, it must have been hard to believe it would someday become a safe, common procedure:

"The first documented cesarean section on a viable patient was performed on April 21, 1610 by Jeremias Trautmann, surgeon of Wittenberg, Saxony. The abdominal wall was stitched close, but not the uterus. The mother survived 25 days, longer than most of the hapless women who would undergo this operation during the next two centuries. Many died promptly of hemorrhage; others, within a week from infection. Rarely did the mother recover. In Paris, for example, cesarean section was performed in 24 patients during the half century 1750 to 1800 without a single maternal survival. So high did feeling against cesarean section run among some groups in that city that they organized an anti-cesarean society in 1797 under the leadership of James Sacombe, and published a journal to help combat the efforts of the operation's advocates… The first successful cesarean section in the United States was performed in 1794, in a cabin near Staunton, Virginia by Dr. Jesse Bennett on his own wife. By 1878 the operation had been performed but 80 times in the United States with a maternal mortality of 53 per cent. It was noted then that the maternal results were better among nine women whose uteri had been gored open by a bull, or who had incised their own abdomen, five of whom survived, than among those who had been operated upon by physicians in New York City, of whom one out of 11 recovered (Speert 2004)."

Safe cesarean births were a phenomenon of the 20th century and then only after the advent of blood transfusions and antibiotics. Indeed, in 16th and 17th century England they had no idea what a germ was. The world had to wait two centuries for Semmelweis and Lister to demonstrate how patients became infected, and another century for the first antibiotic, penicillin. The development of penicillin figured very prominently in the Second World War, as it was to be a life-saving medication for injured soldiers during the Battle of the Bulge. As the first effective medication capable of killing bacteria, penicillin was expensive, scarce, and once administered to the patient, it was rapidly excreted in the urine. Yet it was so crucial to saving lives, that it was often recovered from the urine and reused. As for blood transfusions, they were unknown during the era of William Chamberlen and would not become common until they were used with some frequency during the American Civil War. In William's time bleeding a patient was considered effective therapy. Much of today's knowledge and practices were developed by Dr. Patrick Mollison, "the father of blood transfusions." During the bombing of Britain in World War II Dr. Mollison's contributions in blood-banking were crucial in saving many lives. Combined with skillful anesthesia and good surgical technique, antibiotics and blood transfusions have made cesarean delivery a safe procedure.

In William Chamberlen's era the practice of midwifery was rudimentary. If the mother could not deliver her baby through the vagina, the baby and mother perished. A pregnant woman had many fears as she knew she would be facing a painful labor with certain dangers, including death. She would have to go through birth without the assistance of her husband, for childbirth was exclusively a women's affair at the time. What should have been a happy and joyous experience was commonly fraught with anxiety, fear, and terror. As happy as the mother and father were with the prospects of having a child, the inevitable question always arose: "Could I be the unlucky one?"

An expectant mother would enlist three to six of her female relatives and closest friends to assist her in labor. This group of women knew their responsibilities well, for they either had given birth or knew they inevitably would. They had shared many stories of childbirth and had a good idea of the order of the event, if all went according to the norm. Called "gossips," short for god-sibling, their roles were clearly defined (Wilson 1995). They were to offer support and comfort to the laboring woman. They would talk, chat, and tell stories, many of which were tales of their neighbors and acquaintances. In short, they hovered over the mother, offering her any manner of distraction to help her through the difficult ordeal of increasingly painful contractions. As was the custom, the gossips brewed a special drink called caudle, made with ale or wine and warmed over the hearth with sugar and laced with spices. This concoction would provide the laboring mother nourishment and, depending on the amount of alcohol, some relief from pain.

As the mother-to-be prepared for the birth she contacted a midwife to make arrangements for assistance when her time came. Some midwives were talented and appreciated; others were untrained and dangerous. The only way to tell if a midwife was any good was by reputation. Since midwifery was rife with unskilled, ignorant women who held many superstitions, the death of the mother, baby, or both was all too common.

If all went well the mother had a healthy baby. But when labor did not proceed well and became prolonged the midwife summoned the help of a barber-surgeon. These events always seemed to have a common theme. The mother lay pale and motionless, exhausted by days of labor and dehydration. The darkened room was lit with one or two candles, the air thick with a smell, strong and foul. William knew his responsibility was urgent. With the baby long dead, his task was to keep the mother from the same fate. He knew what to do, and he had brought the instrument in his brown satchel to do it. It was the hook, a long instrument with a handle at one end of the shaft and a large, round,

14

sharp hook at the other. William would pass this up the birth canal, turn it slightly, gaff the baby, and then pull it downwards. It always provided proper traction. Sometimes the baby gradually delivered and other times only parts emerged. One can imagine nothing in his medical experience made William feel more like he had failed than removing a baby piecemeal. Having accomplished this odious task was not the end. Sometimes the mother had heavy bleeding or didn't expel the afterbirth. Occasionally, the mother developed high fever, convulsions, and died. In William's experience, rarely did childbirth result in a healthy baby. On balance, childbirth never seemed to be a happy experience to William.

Not all of William's medical encounters were unhappy. To the contrary, he was a skilled physician who quite enjoyed his practice and helping his patients. Although trained in Paris in medicine and surgery, he far preferred diagnosing and prescribing to surgical procedures. Since William had immigrated to Southampton he was very happy with life in his newly adopted country. His family had many friends in the Southampton Huguenot community and most importantly, they were safe. William enjoyed a modicum of success, although he occasionally was gripped with pangs of regret over leaving his homeland, angry that religious persecution had forced his flight.

Chapter 2   Paris - 1569

William Chamberlen lived in Paris with his wife Genevieve and their three children, Pierre, Simon, and Jane. They led a comfortable life: William, as a respected physician, and Genevieve as the mistress of a busy and growing household. William, the son of a French sea captain, had 22 brothers and sisters. He was now moderately well off financially, and his only problems stemmed from religious persecution he suffered as a Huguenot. Religious and political turmoil would soon determine his fate.

France in the middle 1500s was a Catholic country ruled by a Catholic monarch, Henry II. Catholic churches were at the core of most communities, but that did not mean there would be no incursions from other religions. Martin Luther published his famous 95 theses in 1517, opening the door to the Protestant Reformations. Two decades later, in 1536, John Calvin, a French theologian, published *Institutes of the Christian Religion*, rejecting the authority of the Pope and establishing the doctrine of predestination. He was run out of the country for his contrary views. Settling in Geneva, Switzerland, he promulgated one of the enduring Protestant religions of the world, Presbyterianism. His doctrines of Predestination, in which one's actions were not as important as what the Almighty had in His plan, spread rapidly throughout Europe. No small part of his allure was the anti-Roman sentiment. Calvinism was highly critical of the Roman Catholic religion, particularly the focus on rituals and the obsession with death. He espoused doing away with the Pope and running the church by a system of elders (in Greek *presbyteros*). This idea was soon to be successful in Scotland. Calvin also taught that one should strive for a true Christian society by practicing good works, using charity, humility, and faith as building blocks.

The popularity of Calvinism in France was demonstrated by as many as two million people, or 10 percent of the population, joining the faith. Churches sprang up all over the country. Huguenots were Calvinists from France who spoke a French-based dialect. Walloons were French-speaking refugees from the dominions of Spanish King Philip I, ruler of what today is Belgium. The origin of the term "Huguenots" is explained by Henri Estienne in 1566 in the introduction to his *L'Apologie pour Hérodote* (Encyclopedia Britannia 2002). The Protestants of Tours, France used to assemble at night outside the gates of the palace of King Hugo. In a sermon, a monk declared that these Lutherans should be called Huguenots as kinsmen of King Hugo. The nickname became a popular reference for French Protestants from 1566 onward.

Though most of the Calvinists were peace-loving, some openly attacked Catholicism, desecrating monasteries, convents, and religious icons. Most concerning to the monarchy was that Calvinism was readily adopted by the upper classes and royalty of France. As Calvinism spread rapidly throughout France, this concentration of power became a threat to Catholic establishments, leading to conflict. With eight civil wars erupting and smoldering from 1562-1598, William's greatest concern became the safety of his family. Huguenots had so many insults and threats hurled at them that they began to leave the country in droves.

Henry II died in 1559, needlessly, from a jousting wound, resulting in an era in which his three sons in turn ruled France weakly and ineffectually. The oldest, Francis II, lived but a year after ascending the throne. He was succeeded by his brother, Charles IX, then only 10 years of age, who ruled France until his death in 1574. The third brother, Henry III, then reigned until he died in 1589. Their mother, the Florentine Queen Catherine d' Medici was the true power behind the throne for most of these years, but although she effectively controlled her sons, she could not control France (Dunn 1999).

France was in the seventh year of a civil war between the Catholics and the Huguenots. The atmosphere in France was everywhere tense and dangerous, far too dangerous for a Huguenot family seeking only to live in peace. William and Genevieve loved their home, their neighborhood friends, and their city. This is not to say that their lives were free of care. For devout Huguenots, life in France during the reign of Charles IX meant constant harassment and persecution. Huguenots sensed that the hostility toward their religious beliefs was increasing. They had begun to note that people they passed on the street would not respond to their greetings. Even in the neighborhood shops, they had a gnawing sense that they were being ignored. Catholics were always tended to first, while Huguenots were made to wait.

Outside their home, life was growing intolerable as bigotry, hate, and resentment surged around them. William was convinced that they should move to a land where they would be free of religious persecution. He often raised the topic with growing urgency, but Genevieve was soon to have a baby and understandably she did not want to uproot the family. William probably agreed to abide by Genevieve's wishes for a time, though he did not relinquish the thought that someday an exodus from France would be necessary. As an educated man he certainly had a clear idea where they might go: England, a country receptive to protestant refugees.

He knew that 35 years earlier, when King Henry VIII of England wanted to divorce his wife and the Pope had refused to let him, the King had broken away from Rome and created the Church of England, of which the Parliament had promptly declared him the head. At first, except for the replacement of Pope by King and Latin by the English tongue, the Church of England had retained much of the theology and practice of the Roman church. But when young Edward VI, at age 9, succeeded his father, his advisors had steered England on a more Protestant course. This course had then been reversed briefly when Edward died in 1553 at age 15 and was succeeded by his older sister, Mary Tudor, daughter of King Henry VIII and Catherine of Aragon. Determined to root out the Protestant heresy that had consumed England, the queen who would be remembered as "Bloody Mary" returned England to the Catholic fold and condemned 300 Protestants to be burned at the stake. Her reign lasted five years, until her own death brought her sister Elizabeth to the throne.

Young Queen Elizabeth, wise beyond her years, had steered a middle course, turning the Church of England back toward Protestantism while carefully retaining some of the sacraments of Catholicism, as well as a hierarchy of bishops and archbishops. Yet, at the same time, she remained tolerant of English followers of John Calvin, "Puritans" who would have preferred to banish the bishops and institute a Presbyterian system like that already established in Scotland.

England, during the long rule of Queen Elizabeth from 1558 to1603, was a stable country with strong appeal as a haven for Protestants fleeing religious persecution. The Queen masterfully kept in balance a Parliament divided between a predominantly Protestant House of Commons and a Catholic House of Lords. It thus remained a destination for Huguenots such as William Chamberlen despite continual threats of invasion from abroad and plots from within.

Many Huguenots crossed the English Channel immigrating to England, often settling in Southampton, a major port of entry. Many more migrated farther north and settled in east and west London in areas called Spitalfields and Soho. They tended to remain in a close community, speaking French and not assimilating into the English society. They suffered considerable criticism and prejudice and were referred to as "strangers." But, they were hardworking, law-abiding people who made many contributions to the growing economy of England. Indeed, Spitalfields became a major textile center of Europe, famous for its silks.

Churches were important religious and social centers to these immigrants. The most prominent were the older French Church of London, Threadneedle Street in the east, and later Savoy Church in the west. The east community comprised mainly weavers, artisans, naval officers and ministers. The west community comprised intellectuals, artisans, tradesmen, jewelers, tailors, clockmakers, shoemakers and army officers.

Numerous countries were important havens for the Huguenots. These religious refugees fled to the Netherlands, Ireland, South Africa, and the New World. The first Huguenots fleeing religious persecution left France in 1562 under the leadership of Jean Ribault. In 1564 they established a small colony on the banks of St. Johns River in what today is Jacksonville, Florida. Another colony was soon established in South Carolina. Later colonies were established in New Netherlands, subsequently incorporated into New Jersey, New York and the 13 colonies. These Huguenots made major contributions as weavers, tradesmen, and artisans and even helped to craft their adopted nation. One Huguenot colonist, a Boston silversmith named Apollos Rivoire, later anglicized to Paul Revere and gave his son, who would play a sentinel role in American history, the same name. Eight American presidents have proven Huguenot ancestry: George Washington, Ulysses S. Grant, Franklin D. Roosevelt, Theodore Roosevelt, William H. Taft, Harry S. Truman, Gerald R. Ford, and Lyndon B. Johnson. Any country should be proud to have such immigrants migrating to their shores.

Life for the Huguenots continued to deteriorate in France. Catholic priests had ordered a new round of persecutions. From the pulpits of countless local Catholic churches throughout France priests systematically raged that Huguenots were evil and that all faithful Catholics should rise up and eradicate these infidels. The message could not have been clearer. It had become even more dangerous to be a Huguenot during the civil uprisings in this rabidly Catholic country.

It was the first day in July, 1569, when William and Genevieve, then eight months pregnant, gathered their children and prized possessions, bundling all into a waiting carriage and fled. Can you imagine Genevieve's angst since she was eight months pregnant? William certainly had many conflicting emotions about leaving his homeland and concerns for his family's future. He had no way of knowing that he was to be the patriarch who would catalyze changes in childbirth practices for the world.

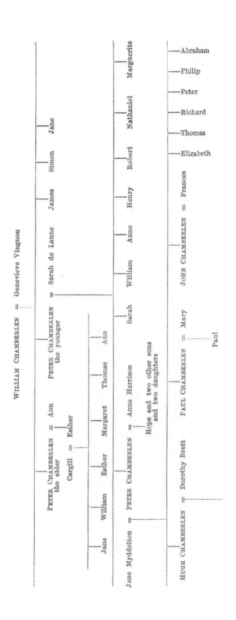

Pedigree of the Chamberlens
(Aveling 1882)

Chapter 3   Southampton - 1569

Southampton, a protected harbor situated on a major English Channel estuary, is near Winchester, the original capital of England some 12 miles north on the River Itchen. In the 12th century the capital was moved to London approximately 70 miles from Southampton.

Once a Roman seaport, Southampton has experienced rising and falling fortunes throughout its history. The original town, relocated to the other side of the River Itchen, was called Hamtun, and home to approximately 4,500 people, mostly wool weavers, craftsmen, carpenters, and blacksmiths. During the early part of the Tudor period (1485-1603) the economic fortunes rose on the robust shipping trade with Italy, which started to decline early in the 16th century. Southampton's monopoly of the shipping trade of tin and lead ended in 1531, adding to the economic decline, yet offset somewhat by the wine trade with France. Then, in the 1560s the influx of Calvinist religious refugees (called Walloons) from Belgium established Southampton as a manufacturing center for serge cloth, giving a boost to the economy.

Southampton has been significant in recent history as the initial departure site of the *Mayflower* in 1623, launch site for the maiden voyage of the ill-fated *RMS Titanic,* point of equipping and transporting of 8 million troops to the continent in World War I, and site of staging and departure of a massive armada for the Normandy invasion on D-Day. In post-World War II Southampton has been a major port for ocean liners and shipping of wool, fruits, cars and containers.

For the Chamberlen family the town was ideal. The population numbered approximately 4000, many of whom shared their plight, fleeing from religious persecution in France and Belgium. The policies of Queen Elizabeth were welcoming to these refugees and they, in turn, were hardworking, skilled craftsmen who were law-abiding, and obviously very religious. Affordable homes, wide variety of available goods, and most importantly a sense of safety made the departure from their motherland less unsettling.

On July 3, 1569 the Chamberlens' ship rounded Portsmouth, turned northwest, and headed into the harbor at Southampton. One can only imagine how difficult this journey was for Genevieve who was only two weeks away from delivering her baby. The ship anchored in the harbor safely and without further incident, and the passengers and their belongings were then loaded onto a smaller boat to be taken ashore. Once ashore and deposited in their new lodgings, William hurried the family off to the tiny St. Julien Church to praise the Lord for a safe, if tumultuous, voyage. It was in this same church that their newest baby Jacques would be christened just three weeks later.

With the family settled, William turned his attention to the business of earning a living. William's knowledge and talents were soon put to good use, assuring his enterprise a favorable start. He did not need to obtain a license to practice, for Southampton was outside the jurisdiction of London. Several Huguenot physicians, all members of his St. Julien Church, became his colleagues and close friends. Initially small, his practice grew rapidly over the next two years as his reputation as a skilled physician spread. Thus established, William was able to earn a modest living, while Genevieve and the children enjoyed the safety of their new home and their adopted country.

In February, 1572, three years after their arrival in Southampton, the Chamberlens again required the services of a midwife as Genevieve bore her fifth and last child. He too was christened Peter, like his 12-year-old brother, who served as a witness to his birth. Curiously, there were now two sons named Peter: Pierre, or "Peter the Elder," who was born in Paris and immigrated to England with his family, and "Peter the Younger," born in Southampton.

By this time, the French king, Charles IX, was twenty years old but in poor physical and mental health. He had been crowned at age thirteen after the death of his elder brother, Francis II, as was the custom in France. He had proved an ineffectual ruler, even with the guidance from behind the throne of his shrewd mother, Catherine d' Medici. But his prospects brightened as the eight-year civil war between the Catholics and Huguenots appeared to resolve by a truce in 1570, a year after the Chamberlens had fled Paris for Southampton. Upon hearing that hostilities had ceased, William likely regretted having left his homeland. But as the months went by and the family continued to prosper in peaceful Southampton, he probably became convinced that he had made the right decision for his family. Events were soon to confirm that he had.

In Paris, following the truce, Catherine d' Medici was continuing to play the role of peacemaker. Through her son, King Charles IX, she announced the marriage of her daughter, Margaret of Valois, to Henry Bourbon, Duke of Navarre. The most eminent Huguenot in France, the Duke was next in line for the throne should Charles IX die childless. The marriage, a symbol of reconciliation between Catholics and Huguenots, was planned for August 1572.

As Paris bustled with preparations for the grand event, Huguenot leaders who had not set foot in the capital for many years came to participate in the festivities. All recognized that this union of Valois and Bourbon held the promise of establishing a lasting peace. But that was not the desire of everyone, in particular the Duke of Guise, foremost of the Catholic leaders in the civil war. To his evil and scheming mind, the gathering of so many prominent Huguenots in one place would provide a unique opportunity to end their heresy for all time. A well-planned assault would turn the truce into a military triumph for the

25

Catholics. In addition to being bold and ruthless, the Duke was a very persuasive man, and in due course he succeeded in convincing Catherine di Medici and King Charles IX to support his designs. In the meantime, the wedding proceeded with Catherine's blessing on August 18, 1572.

On August 23, 1572, St. Bartholomew's Eve, the bells of L'eglise St. Germain l'Auxerrois in Paris began pealing wildly, a signal to the members of the Catholic party to assemble their forces. The next morning, aided by Catholic clerics, they began to hunt down and slaughter the Huguenots. Admiral de Coligny, the Huguenot leader, was among the first to be arrested and executed on the spot as an unrepentant heretic. That day in Paris, 3,000 Huguenots met the same fate as they were dragged from their beds and murdered. The carnage quickly spread to the provinces, and soon blood ran freely in the streets throughout France. In the three weeks that followed, some 50,000 Huguenots were slaughtered in a hate-driven rampage (Dunn 1999).

Safe in Southampton, Peter the Elder, as oldest son, would by tradition follow his father's footsteps and become a physician expecting to inherit his father's practice. Accordingly, from age 14, William started to teach him the "art and science" of medicine. William's training in Paris had included studies of all the medications known at that time, and his skills in prescribing them were without peer. In addition, he could perform most of the common operations, as needed, though surgery was not his preference. Peter, in contrast, methodical and facile with his hands, seemed to relish the operative side of the practice. Furthermore, and curiously, he seemed to be most intrigued by what William considered the least attractive side of his practice: helping a midwife in trouble.

William meticulously taught him midwifery. Every delivery provided a teaching experience for William and his son. The fast labors are the ones in which the baby comes out facing the floor. When the baby is facing up, the labor is slow and sometimes becomes obstructed. First babies take longer in labor than second or third babies. Watch out for the mother who has delivered many babies; she could have a very swift labor. When the afterbirth is delivered, it is important to massage the uterus through the mother's abdomen to decrease the chance of flooding or excessive blood loss after delivery.

By 1580, Peter was 20 years old. His manner was direct and affable, and he had acquired a commanding presence. Peter had not yet taken a wife, but it had not escaped his notice that there were many eligible prospects for marriage in Southampton. When he turned his head at church on Sundays, he could see several beautiful young women in every direction. In the Huguenot community, church service was a common vehicle for young people to meet their future spouses. A particular young woman with a beguiling smile and beautiful dark eyes had not only caught his attention but caused him to glance repeatedly in her direction. Anne Bellechere, who sat in her family pew one row behind him on the opposite side of the aisle, had also been looking in his direction. In the Huguenot Community proper introduction by the families of marriageable young people was a welcomed practice. So it is not surprising that by 1584, we find Peter age 24, happily married and the new father of a daughter, Esther. By this time he was well ensconced in practice and enjoying his work. About this time William decided to introduce Peter's younger brother to the art of medicine. Peter the Elder had been such a success and source of pride to him that it is likely William looked forward to the new challenge.

Over the next year, it was not unusual to see the two men and a boy traveling through the streets of Southampton to visit patients. Although William and Peter commonly worked independently, they relished every chance they had to work together, particularly when they could involve young Peter. Peter the Elder still did not have the experience or the reputation for deliveries that his father had earned. Therefore, whenever the midwives requested William's service, Peter eagerly took advantage of the opportunity to accompany him.

William enjoyed teaching his sons, who both learned quickly. By now young Peter was spending all of his spare time with his father while he administered care to his patients. William always listened carefully to his sons' thoughts, impressed with the intense interest they showed and the alacrity with which they both learned. He taught them to use the fillet, inserting it into the birth canal and looping it over the baby's chin or the buttocks. He showed them how pulling it down and outward by the handles helped babies to descend properly in the birth canal. This instrument certainly was kinder than the hook.

Although Peter the Elder practiced Physick, which included diets, purges, bleedings, and prescribing of medications, all learned from William, he predominantly continued to practice surgery while starting to consult on difficult deliveries. He soon developed a reputation for managing trauma, and in Southampton, a busy seaport, that opportunity commonly presented itself.

In those years, Spain and Portugal dominated the seas and claimed a monopoly on trade with the New World. In addition to transporting the riches that were found there, they would sell slaves they had obtained in Africa to planters in the West Indies, at great profit. However, control of the oceans was not to go uncontested. Before long, clever English sea captains such as Sir Francis Drake and Sir John Hawkins were using their seafaring skills and swifter vessels to waylay the Spanish ships, plundering their gold and treasures. Since the English queen, Elizabeth, both supported and profited from the voyages of these privateers, King Philip II of Spain determined to put a stop to this menace by building a powerful naval fleet and invading England.

Thus it was that in 1588 an armada of some 130 Spanish ships sailed up the Channel bent on conquest of the island. These massive Spanish galleons were an awesome sight, the most powerful fleet the world had yet seen. But the English seamen were ready with their smaller, faster, and better-armed warships. The fierce fighting lasted nine days. In the end the English fleet dispersed the Armada, sinking many and chasing the rest of the heavily damaged galleons back to Spanish waters.

During this great battle, the English ships used Southampton as a supply port, almost always arriving with wounded sailors on board. The many visits of the ships gave Peter, now 28, the opportunity to sharpen his skills at treating trauma, including amputations. Young Peter, now just 16, already somewhat skilled at surgery and use of medications from the tutelage of his father and older brother, also attended the injured. Young Peter became adept at cleaning wounds and scraping away dead tissue from them. He also learned to identify which tissue was so damaged that gangrene had set in. In such cases, he knew that amputation was the only life-saving treatment.

Young Peter would identify sailors for whom an amputation might be needed and presented them to his older brother. Then they would examine the extent of the gangrene and discuss whether amputation was necessary. If so, they would give the sailor copious amounts of rum along with other pain relievers, such as opium, when available. Then young Peter and three seamen would hold the sailor down on a table while Peter performed the amputation. The scene was gruesome as the sailors would struggle, rant, and scream from the agonizing pain. They soon learned that the most important aspect of this procedure was effectively holding down the patient during the operation. Yet, as disturbing as these experiences were to the young surgeons, they knew they were saving lives while honing their skills.

After the decisive English victory over Spain, no one dared challenge England's supremacy on the seas. In the years that followed, England grew in wealth and power and enjoyed a Golden Era in which literature and theater flourished.

Over time, the skills of the brothers in delivering babies also grew, and before long midwives were summoning them for help once or twice a week. The cases they attended were always difficult. Although the brothers probably could perform uncomplicated deliveries better than the midwives, they never had the opportunity. Expectant mothers always chose a midwife or a knowledgeable female friend or family member to perform the delivery since it was unheard of to engage a male for such services. The brothers thus saw only mothers for whom midwives had exhausted all their options but remained unable to deliver the baby.

The brother's entry into midwifery posed a curious situation. William was trained in medicine and surgery in Paris and educated his sons in both disciplines. Why they gravitated to midwifery is hard to explain. The field certainly created prohibitions and barriers for males since they only saw patients by default. Barber-surgeons came to the aid of midwives in difficult situations but they generally spent the bulk of their activities in other aspects of surgery. Dr. Willughby, an Oxford educated physician, was a notable exception who will enter this story years later. He was a physician who practiced as a man-midwife traveling to help midwives in trouble. As we shall see, the Chamberlen men progressively gravitated to almost exclusively midwifery practices.

Another contemporary of the Chamberlens, Dr. Simon Forman (born 1552 – died 1611) grew up just 20 miles to the north in Salisbury. Simon Forman kept a careful diary providing us with a window into conditions in the late 1500s and the early 1600s and the world into which the Chamberlens would enter.

Following the death of his father, Simon worked a decade as an apprentice to a merchant and he developed an interest in herbs as a means of cures. At age 20 he left Salisbury to live with cousins in Oxford where he had a teaching job. He attended Magdalen College Oxford for one and a half years studying medicine and astrology but did not receive a diploma. He returned to Salisbury to practice medicine. The censors of the College of Physicians were not the only people on the lookout for unlicensed physicians. In June 1579 the city clerk and Justice of the Peace on Salisbury, Giles Estcourt hearing of a new doctor with a lucrative practice on the outskirts of Salisbury looked into the matter. He arrested Dr. Simon Forman: "Determined to make an example of the upstart from the farmyard, Estcourt had him committed to prison for sixty weeks. It was sixty weeks before Forman was allowed to petition the queen and the Privy Council" (Cook 2001).

Simon moved to London in 1583. With no diploma or license he was always at the fringe of medicine. His practice of astrology always placed him at odds with the College of Physicians who cited him many times for transgressions. He tried repeatedly over two decades to get a license to practice from the College and even from the Bishop of Canterbury. Then, surprisingly, in 1603 the University of Cambridge awarded him a license to practice medicine, which, of course, would be good for London and all of England. This was due to Simon's 20 years of medical studies and his valiant work in fighting the plague in 1593 when most other physicians fled London in fear. In the background, two advisors to the King requested the licensure. Simon was then able to enjoy the esteem that his prominent practice and intellect had earned.

Meanwhile in Southampton, William still enjoyed teaching his sons, although they had grown in knowledge until their skills had begun to approach his own. In the evening they often discussed the state of medical practice in

England, along with the news from other countries. Their experience with the midwives in Southampton was varied, they found. Some, like their family midwife, were bright and eager to learn. Others, often countrywomen from the surrounding farmlands, did not aspire to greater skills.

Since Southampton was a port city they were prone to hear tales from afar. For instance: "in Germany, a Dr. Muelder became concerned when several of his patients experienced complications and even died in childbirth. He shaved his beard and disguised himself as a woman to attend a delivery so that he could find out what was going wrong. When it was discovered that he was a man invading the women-only sanctity of childbirth, he was brought before a church tribunal, found guilty, and burned at the stake" (Burton 1962). The Chamberlens probably felt physicians were not much better off in England since they were not welcome in a woman's bedchamber to assist at childbirth until a problem had reached the stage when it is almost hopeless.

Chapter 4   Peter the Younger Goes To London - 1594

As young Peter turned 22, he found himself yearning to experience life beyond Southampton. Since he was not the oldest son, he knew he would not inherit his father's practice. Eager to start his career, he decided to move up to London to pursue his own practice.

London is situated on the north bank of the Thames. The City, at the time comprising less than a square mile, lay within walls built during the Roman occupation more than a thousand years earlier. Entry to the city was through one of the nine gates, which guards closed late at night. From the south only one route gave access to the city: the London Bridge. The river Thames dominated the city landscape, providing the chief form of transportation and a major source of livelihood and serving as the ever-changing vibrant backdrop to the city. Three quarters of the trade of England came through London. The prevailing winds were from the south and west, occasionally cleansing the fog and soot-laden air of this bustling commercial center. The population was approximately 200,000 souls, and was judged to be expanding rapidly.

London was pulsating with humanity as rich and poor played out their roles. There were bankers, brokers, merchants, lawyers, military officers, medical men, and members of Parliament comprising the upper ranks of affluence and society. At the other end of the spectrum were the seamen, laborers, hawkers, venders, and craftsmen - all working and all holding together the fabric of this vast commercial enterprise. But then there were the omnipresent poor, the pitiful beggars. The vagrants, rowdies, thieves, and prostitutes were all too common and made it necessary to be on one's guard to avoid becoming a victim.

London was the center of English wealth and power, a magnet drawing in a constant stream of people from the country— youth coming right off of farms arriving in the city with little direction and scant belongings, expecting to be lucky enough to share in these riches. The fates that befell these unsuspecting bumpkins are too cruel to relate. There were always many who wanted to part them from their money. In short, London was not a place for the naïve.

In the case of Peter the Younger, he was well equipped to tackle the challenges of London. He was well educated, stylishly dressed and had good judgment and know-how. Though he was not rich, he had sufficient money to establish himself in London even if it took several months. Obviously, his father had the sophistication to teach his son the ways of the world. Indeed, much of what he was to experience in London his father had already warned him about.

Young Peter found a suitable flat on Blackfriars Lane, just four blocks from Blackfriars Landing on the Thames. This area had once belonged to the Blackfriars' Monastery and now was becoming a neighborhood of family homes. Peter immediately began inquiring about prospects for practice in London. He learned that the Royal College of Physicians, established in 1518 by royal charter of King Henry VIII and now the pinnacle of medicine in England, had an iron grip on the practice of medicine in the City of London and for seven miles surrounding it.

He quickly learned that the prospects of becoming a physician were dismal at best since the Royal College of Medicine insisted on a university degree in medicine, generally from Oxford or Cambridge. But, of course, he didn't have a university education and didn't have the means to get one. Alternatively, he could have attached himself as an apprentice to a practicing surgeon for seven years and be licensed by the Barber-Surgeons Company. That was a long time and all depended upon the vagaries of one man vouching that you were ready to be licensed by the Barber-Surgeons. Having practiced medicine and surgery in Southampton put Peter at a distinct advantage. He would go directly to the Barber-Surgeons Company and request to become a qualified candidate on the basis of his education and practice experience with his father and older brother. Of course, he would have to take an examination, but he was confident that his knowledge base was strong. Accordingly, he applied for entrance to the Barber-Surgeons Company, describing his extensive experience in his father and brother's practices in Southampton. Shortly thereafter, he was summoned to the Barber-Surgeons Hall on Monkwell Street, where his skills and knowledge were rigorously examined. Because he had been so well tutored by his father and brother, this experience proved not very difficult for him, and just three weeks later he received notice that he had been admitted to the Barber-Surgeons Company. Peter at once sent word of his acceptance back to Southampton, thanking his father for all that he had taught him. Next he obtained the red striped pole, with a basin on its end that was the sign of the barber-surgeon. The red stripes were symbolic of the bloody rags that were hung on the pole to dry. Peter displayed it proudly in front of his home on Blackfriars Lane.

Peter well understood the rules of the Barber-Surgeons Company. He knew he could not prescribe medications, as he had done freely and skillfully under the guidance of his father and brother in Southampton, where he was beyond the reach of the College of Physicians. But London was a busy place, and there was so much work for a qualified barber-surgeon that there was little reason for him to be tempted to break the rules. His chances of success in his trade appeared highly favorable, and his prospects for wealth and respect assured.

Barber-surgeons in London, as in Southampton, normally had little to do with childbirth except by default when summoned by a midwife to extract a baby, dead or alive, by means of a traumatic procedure. For them to be involved in childbirth otherwise would require two colossal changes: first, the entrance of a male into an all-female setting; and second, the inclusion of a person educated and trained in the entire birthing process. The result would be a transformation of the childbirth experience which at this time seemed very improbable.

The midwives performed almost all deliveries in London and surprisingly the Bishop of London granted all midwifery licenses. But for midwives, unlike physicians and barber-surgeons, examination of skills and knowledge before licensing was lacking, and visitation and evaluation of services of the licensed midwives were infrequent at best. Even had there been time for such scrutiny, the clergy were ill prepared to provide it. As matters stood, they could never have risen to the task of referring to, or allowing for, illustrations of the generative anatomy. The midwives were therefore loosely licensed, poorly instructed, and unsupervised. There was no way to assure they had even a modicum of education about the process of labor and delivery except by the testimonies of other midwives.

The Episcopal system was directed to provide childbirth services to the women of the 119 parishes of the City and to assure that proper baptism would follow. Since many babies were delivered in situations where it was impossible to get them to a clergyman for a baptism, midwives were also authorized and encouraged to perform the ritual.

Finding a midwife could be simple if the mother chose to use ones assigned to her parish. That was not always the case, for the level of talent varied so greatly that the expectant mother might wish to hire another whom she had heard was more able. At this time, many midwives had come to London from the countryside with no more birthing experience than delivering lambs or calves. Others had witnessed childbirth of their family and friends and decided to take up the trade. If the midwife was trained at all, it was generally by an apprenticeship to a practicing midwife that could last up to seven years. Generally, midwives trained in this way were the most talented. There were no standards, so the mother had to rely on hearsay to discern if a midwife was competent.

Furthermore there were no books available on midwifery and no schools teaching the trade. At this time in England girls generally did not attend schools and most of the midwives were illiterate, thus books would have been of little use. The hiring process was poorly structured, and greatly subjected to the needs and shortages of the parishes. That is not to say that the system didn't work. It just did not work well, and by contemporary standards it was deplorable. Just imagining the Bishop of London instructing the fledgling midwives on generative anatomy or the actual birthing process is comical. There was also the matter of visitation, a process in which the Bishop was responsible for the on-site evaluation of the midwifery skills. This was an even greater comedy, for the visitations occurred sporadically at best and surely presented little opportunity for actual visualization and practical evaluation.

Midwives were usually married women or widows from families of modest means. Most were mature in years, and often were bold and self-confident as they went about their business, whether deserving or not. When Peter arrived in London in 1594, not many midwives could write their names or even make an "X", though by 1634 most of those in London could read, and by 1660 most midwives in England were literate to some degree. This represented a remarkable improvement in a little more than a half century (Wilson 1995).

Husbands, who obviously had a key role in creating the pregnancy, became increasingly less important as pregnancy progressed. Approximately one week before the delivery the expectant mother retired to her room assuming the state of "lying in." There she rested until the time of birth. The husband did not share a bed with her during this time. In some cases the husband even moved out of the home. That is not to say he had no responsibilities, for at the time of labor he had a major role in rounding up the gossips, bringing them to the home where the delivery took place. He would run from house to house collecting all of the gossips (nidgeting) to attend to his wife. This accomplished, his role would be relegated to waiting outside the bedchamber during labor and delivery. The midwife often arrived after the gossips and the birthing process proceeded with no involvement of the husband. If the birth went well the affair could be uplifting and joyous. If labor was prolonged or some other complication set in there was little joy.

In this setting, a typical childbirth could occur with four gossips bustling around the bedchamber as the laboring mother had increasing contractions. When the midwife arrived she would confer a sense of security for she had been through this process many times. She would take over and instruct the gossips as she assessed the progress of the labor. The room was dark with the drapes pulled and a minimum of candle-light. As the pains got stronger the level of hovering by the gossips would increase in an attempt to create maximal diversion for the mother. At the time of birth the midwife might instruct the more experienced gossips to hold the mother's legs while the baby emerged. When all went well, this was a time for womanly triumph and celebration, for a new life had been brought forth, a feat only women can accomplish.

When childbirth did not go well, it was a different matter. A hemorrhage could send the gossips into a flutter; fainting spells were common. When the labor was prolonged for two or three days the gossips often retired or withdrew, leaving the midwife to her devices. After positioning the mother many different ways failed, the midwife would become fearful that she might lose the baby, the mother, or both. That is when she would go to the father and tell him that it was necessary to summon a barber-surgeon. It was general knowledge among fathers that this was only done in extreme circumstances. First, it was almost unheard of to have a male in the bedchamber, and all barber-surgeons were males. Second, the barber-surgeons were known to use drastic measures to remove a baby. So when dire circumstances required these measures, all realized these were desperate situations, for barber-surgeons would use an instrument they referred to as "the hook" to gaff the baby and pull it out, dead or alive, with great injury. A last resort measure to save the mother, it commonly left her with serious injury to the birth canal. Is there any wonder expectant mothers were fearful?

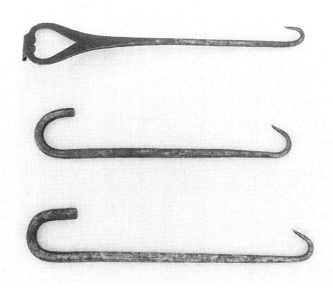

Midwifery Hooks (Courtesy of the Royal College of Obstetricians and Gynaecologists)

Chapter 5   The Royal College of Physicians and Barber-Surgeons Company

At the apex of the London medical hierarchy was the Royal College of Physicians. Established in 1518 by royal charter of King Henry VIII, by 1595 it was the pinnacle of medicine in England. The College, as set down in its founding charter, was to grant licenses to those qualified to practice medicine and to punish those engaging in malpractice as well as unqualified practitioners; these latter included apothecaries and barber-surgeons, as well as errant physicians. An Act of Parliament eventually would extend the College's influence and licensing powers from London to the whole of England. In England

> "there was a great range of other practitioners: wise women and "white witches", skilled herbalists, bonesetters and the midwives. Others generally recognized as "doctors" had learned their skills, like Paracelsus, from reading widely and working, and were generally good medical practitioners. But to be fair to the College of Physicians, there were also a large number of quacks and charlatans skilled only in parting people from their money; necromancers who claimed to tell the future by raising the spirits of the dead, and alchemists claiming to turn base metal into gold – for a price. So there was good reason to bring some discipline into the practice of medicine (Cook 2001)."

Only members of the College were sanctioned to practice Physick and prescribe medicines, and they alone could call themselves "doctors" or "physicians." Membership required a degree from Oxford or Cambridge University and was a coveted honor and distinction. The privileges granted to the College by various charters were as follows:

"1. There is no sufficient Licence without the College Seal.

2. No Surgeon, as a Surgeon, may practice Physick, no, not for any disease, though it be the great Pox.

3. That the Authority of the College is strong and sufficient to commit to prison.

4. That the Censure of the College rising from lesser mulcts to greater, was equal and reasonable.

5. That it were fit to set Physicians bills the day of the Month and the Patient's name.

6. That the Lord Chief Justice cannot baile or deliver the College prisoner; but is obliged by Law to deliver him up to the College censure.

7. That a Freeman of London may be lawfully imprisoned by the College.

8. That no man, though never so learned a Physician or Doctour may practise in London or within seven miles, without the College Licence" (Goodall, 1684).

Members of the College included such luminaries as William Harvey (1578-1657) and Theodore Turquet de Mayerne (1575-1655). William Harvey was physician to three generations of the Stuart family. He was a consummate scientist educated at Cambridge and Padua, and in 1616 he was the first to describe the circulatory system in the human. Many consider him the greatest medical scientist of all time. Théodore de Mayerne from Geneva was educated in Heidelberg and Montpelier. His background was chemistry and he espoused that each disease had specific chemical remedies. He obtained a medical degree from Oxford by incorporation, a courtesy and recognition of his education and eminence. He served as King James I's personal physician and cared for most of the Stuart family. It would be accurate to say that the members of the College of Physicians were the social and educational elite of London.

The Barber-Surgeons Company was one of the early trade organizations in London. Membership in this organization was also strictly guarded, and the Company was in all matters related to medical practice subservient to the College of Physicians. Its members were addressed as "mister" and never as "doctor." They were expected to perform the tasks considered beneath physicians, such as lancing a boil, removing a tumor, or performing an amputation. Barber-surgeons were, however, forbidden to practice Physick; that is, to engage in activities such as ordering diets or purges, performing blood-letting or prescribing medicines. Such transgressions evoked fines by the Royal College of Physicians, or, in severe cases, imprisonment.

The evolution of the barber-surgeons in London requires some explanation. The role of the barber is easily understood, but to understand the association with surgery one must remember that the barbers used finely crafted and sharp instruments. Most of the lesions amenable to early surgical treatment were readily visible on the surface of the body: the wart, mole, sebaceous cyst, boil, and various other growths. The barber, with his sharp instruments, was the best qualified practitioner to remove such lesions. As surgical problems became more complex — for example, amputations or trauma repair — the members required more training and skills. The Barber-Surgeons Company recognized that surgeons must have more extensive knowledge and training. As the surgical aspect of the company developed, it attracted more educated candidates: nonetheless, surgeons never had the honor and respect that physicians commanded.

By the 1590's, when Peter the Younger came to London, the Barber-Surgeons Company had already clearly distinguished the credentials of "barbers" and "surgeons" and they were examined by surgeons to test their knowledge of generative anatomy. Barber-surgeons were progressively being requested, by default, to assist midwives with problem deliveries. They were expected to know about labor, delivery, and the use of all the delivery instruments available at that time.

The usual duration of a labor for a woman having her first baby was 13 hours, though it could be much longer. For subsequent births, the process might last eight hours on average. When labors lasted longer than normal because the baby could not pass through the birth canal, the midwife would summon the barber-surgeon to remove the baby dead or alive.

The barber-surgeon had numerous instruments available. First was the *fillet*, used when the baby was not coming head first. On rare occasions, it was also used when the baby was coming head first but the labor was obstructed. It consisted of a broad band of a flexible material such as silk or leather with rigid handles on each end. The flexible middle portion could be inserted into the birth canal and looped over a fetal part. The handles were then twisted together and pulled to facilitate downward traction for delivery. Next was the *lever,* sometimes called a *vectis*. This long broad instrument, usually curved, was inserted into the birth canal to rotate or, in some instances, to apply downward pressure to the baby. Often fingers were used to apply downward pressure on the baby's skull. Finally, in head-first obstructed labors, the drastic *cranioclast* was actually thrust into the baby's head to collapse the skull. An alternative to this tool was the horrendous *crochet* or *hook* that was so distasteful to William.

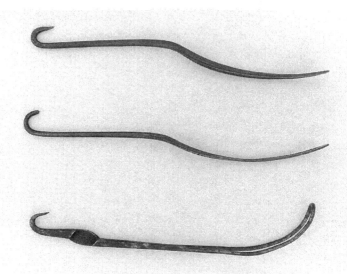

Vectis and Levers with Hooks (Courtesy of the Royal College of Obstetricians and Gynaecologists)

Chapter 6   The Invention - 1595

Peter the Elder remained with his father and concentrated on learning more about difficult deliveries. Evidence that Peter the Elder and his father, William, invented the forceps is strong. That ancient Arabians invented and employed some manner of forceps is not disputed. But what can reliably be stated is at the time of William's practice in Southampton (1569-1596) there were no obstetrical forceps being used in England or the Continent. Furthermore, the first credible evidence of use of forceps was 1733 when Edmund Chapman, country surgeon in Essex, published an account of midwifery forceps indicating that there were several types that had been around for some time. Chapman affirms that the original forceps were an invention of the Chamberlens.

William had long been working on an alternative to what he considered the most repugnant of all his surgical instruments, the hook. Nevertheless, he recognized that it had the distinct advantage of providing proper traction to extract the baby. This property was invaluable in an obstructed labor when a dead baby was stuck in the birth canal. Proper placement of the hook and a tug on it almost always delivered the baby dead, but could also tear the birth canal, endangering the life of the mother.

From time to time the hook delivered a baby that was still alive, but would certainly die. Whenever William had used the hook on a live baby in obstructed labor, it was a procedure of last resort, implemented only to save the mother's life. The results had always been tragic. He did not want to do harm, but that is precisely what the hook did, as it usually caught the baby by the jaw. What was needed was an instrument that enabled him to exert efficient downward and outward traction, combined with the gentleness of a pair of hands placed on the sides of a baby's face in the flat spots between the eyes and the ears. He believed these to be

45

areas on which considerable pressure could be exerted without harm.

I became so intrigued with the process of invention that I decided to try out several possibilities on my kitchen table. It is logical that they would have used simple household items in developing the concept, and that they would have worked at home to protect the secret. I got two large handled, antique serving spoons, the kind used to get the dressing out of a Thanksgiving turkey. These seemed appropriate for the shape of the spoons suggested that they could grasp the baby's head without causing damage. To mimic the baby's head I first considered an orange, then an apple or pear. The orange would not have been a common fruit in 16th century London, but apples and pears were common and readily available. I chose the pear because it had the added property of bruising when ripe. With the assistance of my wife, Carrie, we tried gently extracting the pear from the large woolen ski sock that represented the birth canal.

Carrie held the sock while I attempted to apply the spoon to the pear inside the sock. My first try was clumsy and inept, as my hands and the handles got in each other's way. The spoons were wobbly. The spoons came out, but the pear stayed in the sock. After several attempts, I was able to apply the spoons to the opposite sides of the pear, grasp the handles, pull down and "deliver" the fruit. We felt like we had experienced a little of the mystery of the creation of the forceps. This invention was an event of such historic importance I would like to recreate it as I imagined it to be at that time.

* * *

As William and Peter continued to discuss this problem, the desired instrument began to take shape in Peter's mind.

Delivery of the Pear

He remembered his father serving dinners with two large spoons, held in one hand. He had marveled at how deftly his father had manipulated these spoons, such that he could pick up a single bean or a tiny morsel. He wondered whether such spoon-like instruments could be used in the same way in deliveries. Could they be employed in unison to exert a gentle grasp on the baby's head and then apply downward traction? Peter had already started to measure the size of newborns' heads with a piece of string that he carried to each delivery. He had determined that while the size varied widely from one baby to another, the widest diameter was about 4 inches. Now the only problem was to devise an instrument that could manage an object that large without harm.

Over the following weeks, William and Peter worked by the hearth long into the night, drawing plans with charcoal on large sheets of newsprint. When they decided a plan was not suitable, they crumpled it, threw it into the fire, and began anew. Finally, they conceived a design that seemed to fulfill all their requirements. To test it, one evening they collected from the cupboard two large spoons and a plump pear that was still hard and green. By placing the spoons parallel and facing each other, William was able to grasp the pear and draw it towards him without damaging it or breaking the skin. Peter finished drawing the plan, and they ended that evening contented, confident they had made great progress.

The next two nights they worked on how to grasp the pear strongly enough so that pulling on the spoon handles would not cause the blades to lose their grip and slip off. Peter suggested crossing the shafts of the spoons and anchoring them with a pivot at the crossing point. "Father, in this way we can maintain the pressure of the blades by squeezing on the handles."

William was pleased. "Progress, my son, we have made progress! We should redraw these plans and try again tomorrow night."

Peter immediately sketched their latest concept, discarding the old sketches in the fire.

"Tomorrow night, Father, we shall put this new model to the test. I feel we are getting close."

The next night, Peter brought a woolen stocking to the table. He pushed the pear, now yellowish-brown, midway into the stocking. "Now, Father, your task is to use the instrument to extract the pear from the stocking as if it were a baby's head in the birth canal."

"That appears possible, if I can just slip these spoons around the pear inside the material."

Inserting the spoons one at a time while passing them in a parallel path, William was able to grasp the pear inside the stocking as Peter held it.

"Now pull down gently while squeezing the handles," directed Peter.

The rounded mass began to move along the tube-like upper portion of the stocking.

"And here we are!" gloated William as he delivered the pear to the outside world.

"Again," commanded Peter. "We must try it again."

This time the pear was pushed farther into the stocking. Again William carefully executed the procedure, drawing the pear into sight, the yellow-brown skin glistening in the candle glow.

Then Peter's sharp eyes noted something that troubled him. "Look, Father. The skin is broken and the stocking is wet and sticky. The spoons have broken the skin of the plump pear."

"But the pear is ripe and soft now," said William. "I did not apply great pressure."

"Ripe and soft is why this problem occurred," said Peter. "But it is telling us something important. A baby's skin is soft and fragile. We must shape the blades so that they apply pressure where it is effective for pulling the baby out, but not where it can cause damage. I believe we should hollow out the spoons, leaving just the edges, and those must be rounded."

The two men looked at each other, both nodding "yes" and grinning. Peter immediately started to draw the new design, estimating that a baby's head would be approximately twice the size of their noble, but bruised, pear. They decided on an instrument with two blades and handles, joined at the middle by a pivot, looking like two large, long-handled spoons with their centers missing, connected at mid-shaft.

"It must be slender enough to fit into the birth canal but large enough to grasp the baby's head and pull it down," said Peter.

"Yes. The blades should be fenestrated," added William, "with oval windows about 1 by 8 inches in one and 1 by 5 inches in the other. That will let us grasp the baby's head while not putting too much pressure at any one point."

"Yes, yes," agreed Peter. "That sounds just right."

Peter revised the plans faster and faster as they spoke, for he was confident that they were near success. As he worked, William brought forth a bottle of port and filled two glasses. Peter completed the drawing of the fenestrated blades, locked together with a pivot on one of the shafts. "That does it!" he exclaimed triumphantly.

They cut the pear and ate it, as they drank a toast to their continued progress.

The following day, drawings in hand, the inventors paid a visit to the blacksmith, in his small, dirt-floored shop housed in a lean-to shed near the harbor. He was forging a gate-post over his bucket oven. His face was craggy and sooty, his eyes intently focused, as sparks flew like cascading water under the mighty strokes of his hammer. Finally, he looked up and greeted his visitors with a nod and a grin. William and Peter returned the greeting and told him they had come to ask his help in constructing a special instrument. Before they showed him the drawings, they warned him, this undertaking must be kept secret. The blacksmith vowed that he would never tell anyone anything about it. He scrutinized the drawings, turned to his visitors, and nodded his head. "I can craft this."

Putting aside his other tasks, he worked most of that day and part of that evening forging two fenestrated iron blades that were locked together by a pivot on one.

William and Peter returned the following day and examined the finished instrument. "This is good. It is exactly what we wanted. You must take the jagged edges off though," said Peter.

"Easily done," replied the smith.

The Chamberlens paid him three shillings and thanked him for his good work and for agreeing to keep their secret. They left the blacksmith shop in high spirits, slapping each other on the back, excited over the prospects for their invention.

"I know it is not like the discovery of fire or water," mused Peter, "nor like the invention of the wheel, but it may be a gift that with God's help will save many lives."

"I only hope we will have the opportunity to use it soon," said William.

"Who will use it first?" asked Peter.

"It was your idea. You use it first."

"No Father, you're the teacher, the grand master. You be the one to initiate it."

They expected to have many opportunities to try out the instrument, as William and Peter's services were now requested frequently. But they had to wait for the right circumstances. Above all, they determined that no one must know about the instrument. This would be a trade secret, since it would provide them with the potential to recover the losses incurred by their exodus from France.

* * *

Very likely the first times that they used the forceps it did not work well. This is not surprising, for even today when forceps or vacuum assisted deliveries are attempted by highly trained physicians, they are not always successful. However, it is reasonable to assume that they carefully selected the situations to use the secret instrument and were able to demonstrate the utility of the technique fairly soon, for their success and notoriety was evident by 1600, and by 1604 Peter the Elder was appointed Physician in Ordinary to the King and Queen.

With the invention facilitating their efforts, William and Peter now enjoyed their birthing experiences and their discussions that followed each delivery. They were colleagues and, more important, good friends, so it was particularly disappointing for Peter when William decided

51

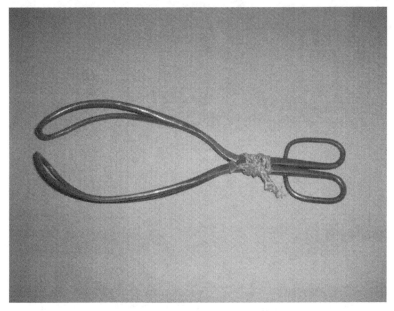

The Original Chamberlen Forceps (Courtesy of the Royal
College of Obstetricians and Gyneacologists)

to retire and spend an extended visit in London with young
Peter. Of course, Peter inherited the Southampton practice
and continued to enjoy great success with the help of the
secret instrument. He had to be on his guard, however, for
concealing the instrument became more difficult without a
partner to distract onlookers. Nonetheless, he managed to
develop an effective routine that would keep the secret safe.

Chapter 7   They Were Doing What?

William and Peter had devised an instrument that was to change childbirth practices, saving countless lives over the centuries. The circumstances were hardly favorable and lesser men would have failed miserably. Practicing in an era when they didn't have their own patients, becoming involved only when the midwife had exhausted all of her skills and the mother and baby lay close to death, was not a propitious way to introduce a new instrument. The success of forceps deliveries lies in the timely delivery of the baby before trauma and damage occur from remaining in the birth canal for extended periods of time.

The introduction and testing of the technique could have been relatively easy if there were no secrecy involved. But, this was not the case. Had it been, the men could have used the device in critical cases when the mother was exhausted and perilously close to death. The technique and the modification of the device could have been achieved with ease. The Chamberlens' decision to keep the instrument a family secret posed great difficulties and presented a preposterous situation, almost comical in itself. Certainly in Elizabethan England the temperament was a little proper and prudish, to say the least. The very presence of a male in the birth-chamber was shocking and contrary to all rules of modesty. The male English midwife, Percival Willughby, wanting to help his erstwhile midwife daughter with a delivery problem, described crawling into a birth-chamber on his hands and knees to escape being noticed by the mother (Willughby 1972).

In this setting the Chamberlen men proposed that the women midwives raise their outer skirts and drape them over the mothers bent knees so they could insert the instrument into the mother's birth canal unseen by her or the midwife herself. The Chamberlens then had to manipulate the forceps to get them properly positioned, which often entailed having the midwife moving right, left, and forward and backwards in what must have looked like a ceremonial birth dance. And finally they had to exert downward and outward pressure to bring the baby out, all done under the midwives' raised skirts.

How did this ever happen in the first place? The best explanation is that the midwives were desperate. They knew if they didn't get help the baby would certainly die and the mother might as well. When they sent for the assistance of the barber-surgeon they were calling for help from someone they knew and trusted. The knowledge and authority of the consulted male were generally far greater than what they had to offer. So it is likely they would have been amenable to doing anything the barber-surgeon requested in this dire situation.

The Chamberlens designed a wooden box built to hide the forceps when they were being transported. The box was slightly bigger than a loaf of bread, but that is where the comparison to a prosaic staple ends. The box was sturdy, ornate and gilded, hardly likely to escape notice. The box would only be opened in the birth chamber after all were required to depart.

As comical as this practice was, it had the potential to change childbirth forever. The forceps shortened labors and saved babies' lives, not to mention the lives of the mothers in prolonged labors. Naturally, the Chamberlens—with their secret instrument—were engaged with increasing frequency in labors until their skills and success became legendary. This opened the door for more trained and skilled barber-surgeons to become involved in childbirth. The evolution that followed was a major benefit for English midwifery, as educated and trained barber-surgeons became increasingly involved in the process of childbirth. This served as a threat or challenge to the midwives to learn more and improve their skills. It culminated a century later with much improved delivery techniques and lying-in hospitals springing up all over London.

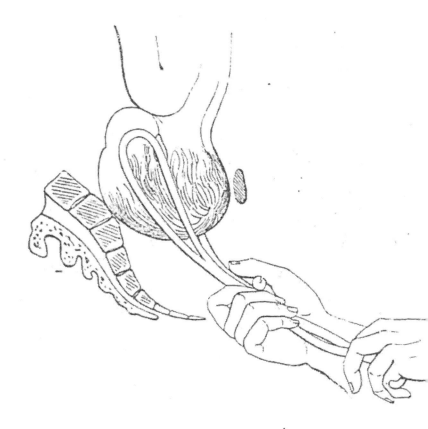

Use of the Forceps (Chailly-Honoré 1864)

TAB XVI

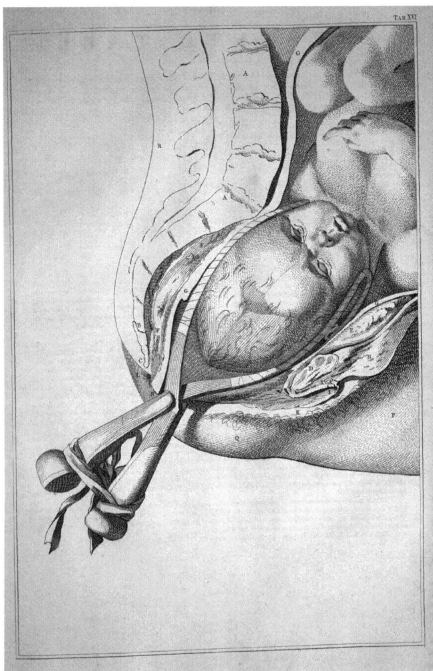

Use of the Forceps (Smellie 1754)

Chapter 8   The Courtship

Peter the Younger had accomplished much during his brief time in London, but one of his greatest challenges still lay ahead: meeting, wooing, and winning the lovely Sarah de Laune.

William de Laune, a French Huguenot clergyman, fled to London with his family to escape religious persecution. An educated man, he sought a degree at Cambridge by incorporation. This was a courtesy afforded by Oxford and Cambridge to allow selected educated men from the Continent to take an examination, and be awarded a degree. When conferred, the degrees were considered on a par with regular degrees. Upon receiving his degree, he decided to become a physician, learning medicine, most likely as an apprentice to a physician. Eventually, he earned membership in the Royal College of Physicians, and became a highly respected physician in London.

Since Huguenots remained in rather tight communities in England, it is reasonable to assume that Peter met the de Launes through his church. William de Laune's wife had died in France, and subsequently he arrived in London with his daughter Sarah and her three brothers. Sarah assumed much of the responsibilities of the household and learned the arts of music, literature, and household management. Her brother, Gideon, was to become a noted apothecary and established the Worshipful Society of Apothecaries in 1617 when it achieved independent status from the Royal College of Physicians. Not much information is available about the courtship of Peter and Sarah, but several points seem clear. First, the romance was fast and effective for they were married soon after he arrived in London. Second, they had an enduring union and Sarah gave him eight children and was continuously helpful as a hostess in their home. Third, as the son of a French immigrant, Peter gained certain acclaim by his association with William de Laune who had reached the respected status of member of the College of Physicians. Finally, it is clear that William de Laune and Peter had many opportunities for discussion of their common interest, medicine.

The wedding was scheduled for May. It was an elaborate affair, with many relatives and London dignitaries attending. Sarah's brother, Gideon de Laune, a wealthy apothecary, was present. Her other brothers, Paul, a merchant, and Peter, a minister at Norwich, also were on hand with their families to witness the marriage. After the ceremony and the feast that followed, William de Laune gave the couple a full purse of money as a wedding gift, a sum that helped considerably shortly thereafter when they bought their new home at 20 Blackfriars Lane (Aveling 1882).

Chapter 9   Peter the Elder to London with Forceps - 1597

On a morning early in 1596, Peter received a message that his father had been struck by a pestilence and died unexpectedly, a tragic loss for the whole family. The best evidence indicates that he died in London, but where he was buried remains a mystery. The likely sites, St Julien Church in Southampton, Threadneedle Street and Savoy churches in London have no record of his death or burial. What is not a mystery is that the loss had profound effect on Peter the Elder.

As the grieving eased, Peter decided it was time to make an important change in his life. He would take the secret to his brother in London, and together they would extend its benefits to a larger population of women while expanding their own practices. Shortly thereafter he moved his family northwards. Settling first in temporary lodgings in East London, Peter soon found a proper home for his family on Mark Lane, west of the Tower of London. The home was equidistant from the London Bridge and the Tower, and a short walk from his younger brother's home on Blackfriars Lane. The area had been settled some years earlier by Huguenot emigrants, many of whom were now prospering as textile workers, jewelers, and craftsmen. Most importantly, there was a Huguenot place of worship nearby, Threadneedle Church, which would be convenient for Peter's small family. The location and accommodations were ideal for a medical practice: a large house with two ground floor rooms suitable for an office and easy access to the homes of potential patients among the Huguenot community.

In 1597, the elder Peter sought to join the Barber-Surgeons Company. His experience in Southampton had provided him with impressive qualifications, and young Peter's membership gave him a distinct advantage. Since

Peter had not worked as an apprentice for a freeman of the Barber-Surgeons Company in London, he had to apply as a "foreigner" to take the oral examination. Each year, the examiners alternated: barber, then surgeon, then barber. At the time of Peter's examination, it was the barber's turn, but in order to have a rigorous test of his midwifery skills, a senior surgeon also examined him on the subject of genital anatomy and difficult labors (Radcliffe 1989).

Peter, now 38, had been superbly tutored by William, and using that instruction, along with his extensive experience in practice, passed the examination with ease and "was promptly admitted to the Barber-Surgeons Company upon payment of a seven guinea fee for the exam, and 20 shillings to the clerk of the Company for his diploma. He made his expected donation of a guinea to the Company poor box and paid his quarterly sum of twenty pence to the Master of the Company. A hood was placed upon Peter's shoulders and he was awarded his striped pole with a basin that he promptly placed in front of his residence on Mark Lane (Radcliffe 1989)." With his brother's reputation affording a great boost to his practice, Peter enjoyed rapid success in London. By this time, Peter the Elder had presented his brother with his own set of forceps that he had paid the blacksmith to forge prior to leaving Southampton. The brothers met frequently, exchanged ideas, and shared what they variously called "the invention" or "the secret instrument." With Peter's help, young Peter soon became skilled in its use. Commonly, the two would attend deliveries together.

The reputation of the Chamberlen brothers spread rapidly throughout London, as their skills in delivery appeared to far exceed those of any other barber-surgeons. Every reference to them included mention of a mysterious device that enabled them to shorten the agony of labor by overcoming obstruction, though it seemed no one had ever seen it. By whatever means, it was recognized that their efforts had resulted in the birth of a live baby from a living mother in many cases when one or both would have been lost. Before long, they began to be known as miracle workers, not only to the midwives but to the rest of the populace.

With increasing fame came also an intense curiosity to learn their secret. To preserve it, the brothers went to extraordinary lengths to conceal its nature. At first, they regularly transported the instrument in a wooden box the size of a long loaf of bread. As news of their success spread so did the curiosity of the onlookers and particularly their competitors. The intrigue of uncovering the mystery and using it to gain riches was compelling to their competitors. To confuse curious onlookers, they decided to create the illusion that the device was very large. Consequently, they ordered the construction of a carved and gilded box, so huge that it required two men to carry it into the bedchamber. On its arrival and before it was opened, the midwife and all attendants would be locked out of the room and the mother would be blindfolded. When they took the instrument out of the box, the brothers would then ring bells and slap sticks together to confuse those present and those outside the locked doors. They even anticipated that the mother might divine something about the instrument from hearing the clanking of metal, so they avoided that possibility by covering the handles with leather.

Fame and success had its price. Three years after joining the Barber-Surgeons Company, Peter was so busy that he frequently failed to attend the lectures mandated by the Company. As a result, he was summoned on several occasions by Company authorities and directed to pay a fine. Since he felt strongly that he knew most of the material in the lectures, he was pleased to learn that he could apply and pay a fee for a "license of absence" from them. He obtained one such license on March 2, 1602, next paying fees

June 9, 1602, and March 13, 1603, for additional licenses of absence (Aveling 1882).

Such expenses were easily borne, since the brothers' services continued to grow in demand, and they prospered accordingly. It was understood by the midwives that the brothers would charge an appropriate fee for their services, and a substantial one compared to the few coins a midwife earned. The midwives usually would tell the expectant father about it when they informed him that they needed to call in help. The Chamberlens were most often paid at the time of the delivery, but the account was always settled by the time of the baptism. Their fees varied from £1 to £3, according to the difficulty of the delivery but also to the means of the patients. Mindful of the powers and the favor they had been granted, they charged nothing if the family was very poor. Such, they believed, was the grace their God would expect of them.

It was the elder Peter who was first recognized by royalty. His skills were widely acclaimed and he was called upon to help numerous ladies with difficult deliveries. Among members of Court word of his good services spread rapidly. Peter became in strong demand in royal circles.

Chapter 10   Dr. Peter's Birth - 1601

On May 8, 1601, a heavy fog rolled off the Thames and lingered throughout the day. The cobblestones on narrow, winding Blackfriars Lane glistened with moisture. The Chamberlen house at 20 Blackfriars Lane, shrouded in a mist, was now disturbed by a sudden air of activity. The charwoman rushed out the door to get the neighbor women and returned hurriedly with them. There was a bustling of people, coming and going.

Sarah had a midwife for her delivery and as much as is known indicates that the delivery progressed well. Peter and Sarah decided to name their baby boy Peter making him the third Peter in the family. Uncle Peter, Anne, and 16-year-old Esther arrived soon after the baby was born. Since they had only a daughter, they were especially delighted now to have a nephew.

There was an order to the days surrounding childbirth, as it was the custom in England then to follow certain prescribed practices. Lying-in occurred in three stages. In the first, a week before the baby was due, the mother retired to her bedchamber. In the second, after the delivery, the mother remained in bed for one day. In the third, the mother was allowed to be up and around, but only in her bedchamber for up to a month, according to her strength. During the five- to six-week period of lying-in, the husband saw to all of the household chores and conjugal activity was suspended (Wilson 1995).

Calvinist Huguenots considered the baptism a very serious affair. It was performed on the fourth day of the baby's life without the mother, for she was still lying-in. This was in direct contrast to the practices of some Anglican families, who, according to Pepys, regarded Christenings as more of a social affair. Of the 16 he describes, but one was in a church, and that was a Huguenot baptism. For middle and upper class Anglicans it became a sign of social success to

63

have the christening in their homes and to choose sponsors for their social importance (Pepys 1970).

Four days after his birth, on May 12, 1601, Peter III was baptized in the French Church on Threadneedle Street in the Parish of St. Anne. The proud father, new aunt and uncle, Ester, and the godparents attended. The midwife and the gossips were also present, as well as Sarah's brother, Gideon de Laune. Sarah was still at home lying-in. Her time would come, for her "churching" would happen soon enough.

Following the baptism ceremony, as was the custom, the godmother, gossips, and the father gave the midwife coins and thanks in payment for her services. The new father, Uncle Peter, Anne, and Esther then returned to Blackfriars Lane for a celebratory dinner.

Next, when the baby was about three weeks old, came the ritual known as "churching of the mother." The mother, who had been absent from the church for some time, appeared before the congregation with her midwife, gossips, and the godparents. In a formal ceremony of thanksgiving, she was reintroduced to the church (Wilson 1995).

For this immigrant family, the christening of a first son would have been a very important event. They had risen in social and professional circles, but the medical system had posed strict barriers. For Peter the Younger and Peter the Elder, this new arrival was their surrogate; they would tutor, guide, and support him to fulfill a dream, unattainable for themselves: the admission to the Royal College of Physicians.

Chapter 11   Royal Births

The Chamberlen brothers acquired their extraordinary reputations and became known throughout London for their ability to deliver babies safely in difficult situations. Their skills were touted so highly that Peter the Elder eventually became a regular attendee at Court. As a result, he and young Peter were engaged to deliver numerous other wellborn infants, enhancing their reputations still further.

It is clear that Peter the Elder knew the King and Queen, and judging from events yet to occur Peter had a very close relationship with the royal couple. King James, now King of England and Scotland, was 39. He was a smallish man with a long narrow face who stuttered when he talked. Queen Anne, at age 31, was blonde and very beautiful, with a fine complexion, matchless social graces, and a penchant for spending money. She became pregnant with her sixth child, Mary, in 1605.

Having a royal birth was a very special affair. Sir Ralph Winwood, born in Northhamptonshire in 1564, served King James I as envoy to Holland. He was knighted in 1603 and served as Secretary of State from 1614 until his death in 1617. His three volumes of collected papers and letters give us an insight to the planning, preparations, and nervous energy expended. A short time before the confinement when the King and Queen were in New Market, Sir Dudley Carlton wrote Mr. Winwood, "Here is much ado about the Queen's lying-down, and great suit for the offices of carrying the white staff, holding the back of the chair, door-keeping, cradle-rocking, and such-like gossips' tricks."

Then when the King and Queen were in Whitehall, Samuel Calvert wrote to Winwood: "There is great preparation of nurses, midwives, rockers, and other officers, to the number of forty or more" (Winwood 1785).

After the royal couple retired to Greenwich as was the custom for royal births, Calvert writes Winwood: "The

Queen expects her delivery every hour, and prayers are dayly said everywhere for her safety. There is great preparation for the christening chamber, and costly furniture provided for performance of other ceremonies." Indeed, among the King's disbursements was an entry of "The Queen's child-bed and other necessary provisions for that time £52,542." To put that amount in perspective, a live-in domestic was paid 2-3 pounds per year at this time.

Winwood received another letter from John Packer: "The Queen is not yet delivered but is come to the end of her reckoning. The midwives are here attending, but she will not speak with any of them till she hath need of their help, neither will she signify which of them she will employ until the easiness or hardness of her travaile doth urge her to it."

A midwife named Alice Dennis attended Queen Anne when she delivered Princess Mary in 1605 in Greenwich. A note dated May 28, 1605, outlines her compensation. "To Alice Dennis, midwife, the sum of £100 for her pains and attendance upon the Queen, as of his Highness' free gift and reward, without account, imprest, or other charge to be set on her for the same." As we shall see she was one of several midwives in residence available for service, if elected.

The first royal to employ Peter the Elder was Queen Anne of Denmark, wife of James I. She had seven babies and it is clear that he was the Midwife in Ordinary to King James I and Queen Anne, but the actual number of deliveries he attended is less certain. A list of her births follows:

> 1594, Henry – Stirling Castle - died of typhoid fever at 18years
>
> 1595, Elizabeth – Dunferiline, Scotland, the town where Robert Bruce was buried. She had many suitors but married Frederick V, Count Valentine of the Rhine. He was crowned King of Bohemia in 1519 and Elizabeth the Queen two days later. But it was not to last a year, as Frederick was defeated in The Battle of White Mountain and died of an infection.

Elizabeth, known as the Winter Queen, was forced to flee in exile to The Hague.

1598, Margaret – Dalkeith - died as an infant in March of 1600

1600, Charles – Dunfermline - became King Charles I

1602, Robert – Dunfermline – died at 4 months

1603, miscarriage – Dunfermline

1605, Mary – Greenwich - attended by Peter the Elder Chamberlen and Alice Dennis, midwife – died at 2 ½ in Middlesex, England

1606, Sofia – Greenwich Born March 22, died March 23

Peter the Elder did not attend the first five deliveries of Queen Anne because they took place in Scotland. Following the death of Queen Elizabeth on March 24, 1603, James, then Scone of Scotland, proceeded to London to claim the throne of England and Scotland. Queen Anne remained in Scotland and did not come to Windsor Castle until July 2, 1603, when she arrived with seven-year old Prince Henry.

It was clearly established that Peter the Elder became her Royal Midwife in ordinary. Perhaps losing Robert at four months and the Queen's recent miscarriage prompted the King to engage a man-midwife for childbirth. There were only two deliveries that Peter could have attended: Mary in 1605 and Sofia in 1606. Because of his close relationship to the King and the Queen it is likely that he attended both of these deliveries.

The Queen was in the eighth month of a pregnancy that had progressed without complications. It was decided that Peter would be in-residence, beginning at the time of her expected delivery. Since no firsthand account can be found relating this experience, let us create a scenario as it may have been.

* * *

One morning two days before Peter was scheduled to be in residence to await the delivery, a royal coach thundered to a halt at 20 Mark Lane and discharged a grim-faced messenger. A throng of onlookers who had followed the vehicle was assembled outside the Chamberlen home. The royal attendant rapped loudly on the door and announced that Queen Anne requested Peter's presence at once. Peter, knowing there was no time for the large wooden box carried by two servants, quickly retrieved the smaller wooden box with gilt trim, inserted the instrument, and then carried it to the waiting coach, immediately departing for the royal residence in Greenwich, with onlookers in curious pursuit.

Upon his arrival, an aura of excitement descended on the Palace, but Peter also sensed a hint of uneasiness, for this was the first time a male had attended a queen of England in childbirth. Peter was directed to the hall outside the bedchamber, where he was greeted by King James himself.

"Thank you for coming so quickly," sputtered the King. "They tell me the Queen has been laboring since dawn. Her attendants are with her in the bedchamber. The matter is in your hands. I trust everything will go well."

"I am sure it will, Your Majesty," Peter assured the King. "I will give you a report shortly."

"The Queen's choice of the five midwives is Alice Dennis. You will see her in the birth chamber as well as the gossips."

A lady-in-waiting escorted Peter into the bedchamber. The room was darkened, lit only by one of three large chandeliers. The drapes were drawn, and cloths were stuffed into the keyholes of the heavy doors. Peter blinked, but rapidly grew accommodated to the dim light. Everyone fell silent. No less than seven women were attending the Queen, most of them positioned at the head of the bed speaking softly to her and trying to make her comfortable. It was a tense and icy moment for the ladies as they sensed the strangeness of having a male in attendance.

Peter immediately took charge, respectfully greeting Queen Anne and assuring her and the attending women that everything would go well. He nodded to Alice Dennis and she moved aside to let Peter observe his patient. Another contraction started, and the gossips began to chatter with Queen Anne, providing her pleasant distraction from the pains. She looked splendid and unruffled. With each contraction, the attendants intensified their efforts to distract her. Peter observed that the contractions were lasting up to a full minute. Since this was a sixth baby, he knew that the delivery would not be far off.

He had placed the ornate wooden box along an empty wall where it would be safe. After observing the Queen for a few minutes, he turned to her and said, "It appears that your labor is progressing well. After a few more contractions, I will wish to examine you to determine if the baby is coming down properly."

The Queen nodded assent and said, "I think the baby is near because I am feeling pressure deeper in my pelvis."

Peter said, "I shall tell the King that the labor is progressing. I will need some fresh butter and hot water. Who shall fetch that for me?"

Alice Dennis indicated that a gossip would fetch these items immediately. Peter stepped out of the bedchamber and saw an agitated King James pacing and talking to himself. A smile from Peter seemed to put the King at ease. "Labor is going well, Sire, and it will not be very long before we have a baby."

King James smiled. "That is very good news. Thank you, Master Chamberlen. I must admit I have become quite nervous while waiting here."

Peter bowed and re-entered the dimly lit bedchamber.

The gossip returned with the butter and water, and Peter asked Queen Anne if he might examine her now to assess the progress of the baby. She nodded. The attendants immediately deployed in two groups. Five hovered at her shoulders. Two shifted to the bottom of the bed as if the guardians of Queen Anne's modesty.

Peter, sensing the uncomfortable nature of the move, said to the latter two, "You gently hold the Queen's right knee and you gently hold her left knee." The attendants immediately felt better, with their role as Queen Anne's supporters and protectors recognized by this male stranger, who seemed calm and respectful. Peter slowly and carefully inserted the first two fingers of his right hand into the birth canal, using the butter as a lubricant. To his surprise, the baby's head was right there. The Queen tolerated the examination well, but, more significantly, she endured the presence of the baby's head pressing down on her pelvis without any outward display of urgency or pain. "I believe we are ready," Peter said, smiling at Queen Anne. He addressed the attendants again: "Help me position the Queen at the bottom of the bed."

The attendants promptly helped arrange Queen Anne for a delivery. With her next contraction Peter instructed her to bear down with this contraction. The Queen seemed to follow this direction effortlessly. The top of the baby's head could now be seen at the opening to the birth canal. Peter was now confident of the outcome: "We are close. With the next contraction we shall have the baby."

The next contraction came, and Queen Anne pushed again. The head emerged *en caul*. This meant that instead of the membranes rupturing, they remained intact and covered the baby's head as it emerged. Peter was pleased, for this was a sign of good luck. He immediately reached into his satchel for a sharp wooden stick, skillfully pierced the membranes, and pulled them down over the baby's head. The shoulders emerged easily and the baby was delivered. About ten seconds after the delivery, the baby girl let out a hearty cry, announcing to the world that she finally had arrived. After tying and cutting the umbilical cord Peter placed the infant into the waiting arms of Alice Dennis, the midwife, who swaddled her. Anne Dennis then placed the newborn in the open arms of the Queen, who kissed her baby and lovingly inspected her hands and toes. She then held her baby girl close to her breast.

The afterbirth was slow in coming out. Peter, in his wisdom, chose to be patient. He knew that premature or hasty attempts to deliver the afterbirth could lead to heavy bleeding. He waited and chatted with the Queen and waited some more. Finally, Queen Anne gave a concerted push downwards and the placenta emerged. Peter smiled broadly. He inspected the afterbirth for completeness and was satisfied.

"Your Majesty, you have a beautiful girl. The afterbirth is delivered. You do not have any bleeding. It appears that my work is over." He smiled and then added, "Please remain in bed for a day and I shall return then to see how you and the baby are faring."

"Master Chamberlen, I cannot thank you enough. You are very skilled indeed," said the Queen kissing her new baby.

"I shall leave now and will tell the King the good news," said Peter, turning to pick up the gilt wooden box that had never been opened. As he entered the hall, Peter saw the expected royal officials who attest to the delivery sitting around the periphery of the hall. King James came up to him smiling. "Do you have news?"

"Yes, very good news, Your Majesty. You have a healthy baby girl. She was born *en caul* and that is a sign good luck."

"Will she get over this *caul*?" asked the King.

"Oh yes! That just means that the membranes were over her head and not ruptured at the time of delivery. It is a sign of very good luck, Your Majesty."

"I think that is what I had when I was born. But what is in the gilt box?" asked The King.

"That is my special instrument."

"Did you use it on the Queen?"

"Oh, no," replied Peter. "It is only for difficult labors, ones that are prolonged two or three days, and would otherwise not deliver. Your baby delivered very easily. The Queen performed splendidly."

"As did you, Mr. Chamberlen. We had heard that you were the most skillful of man-midwives in England. We are fortunate to have the best."

Peter bowed deeply at the compliment and to signal that he was leaving. "I shall be back in 24 hours to look in on the patients. Send for me if you need me."

He left triumphantly carrying the gilded wooden box.

* * *

Chapter 12   Dr. Peter's Childhood

It would be an omission not to comment on the partnership that raised Peter III. His uncle and his father were both very involved in raising him, his father because that is what fathers are supposed to do. His uncle, however, was inordinately involved and that cannot have been just because he did not have a son. These men were from an immigrant family and had suffered all of the indignities that come with being considered foreigners or strangers in England. They both would have been physicians had they been fortunate enough to have gone to a university. This was their first opportunity to have a physician in the family. They anticipated they would benefit and live vicariously through his success, particularly if this child were to become a member of the College of Physicians. It was to this end that they tutored, taught, prompted, and tended him on a constant basis. In addition, he had a nursemaid who schooled him in the alphabet and a teacher who taught him rhymes, numbers, and the simplest of mathematics.

Sarah described Peter as a beguiling child, alert and sociable. Slightly big for his age, he had curly brown hair, big eyes, a dimple in his chin, and an upturn at each side of his mouth that gave him the appearance of a constant smile. He immediately locked eyes with anyone addressing him, and his manner was easy and confident. Everyone enjoyed being around him, but, of course, that was his mother's assessment.

Peter had seven siblings who shared the attention and love of their doting Uncle Peter: Sarah, born in 1604, William in 1606, Anne in 1608, then Nathaniel, Henry, Robert, and finally Marguerite, the youngest in 1615. Uncle Peter loved all his nieces and nephews, but there was never any question about who was his favorite.

Sarah was generous with her time with each of her eight children, making sure they were proficient in French, had good manners, and were well cared for at all times. She insisted that they be properly dressed, especially for dinner, and that they always greeted visitors to their home most cordially. As the two oldest, Sarah and Peter frequently received fashionable new clothes sewn or knitted by Sarah while their siblings got the hand-me-downs. They were blessed to have a mother like Sarah.

His parents provided the best instruction in deportment and manners for their children. Following the French tradition, Sarah insisted that each of them, as soon as they could sit at the table, should dine with the family; that is, after they had scrubbed their hands in the table basin that stood prominently at the doorway to the dining room.

Uncle Peter frequently visited and doted on his nephew. Peter, as a mere five-year-old, accompanied him on a visit to see a man who had had a benign tumor removed from his scalp a week before. By the time he was seven he had made a score of home visits with Uncle Peter, now his teacher and mentor. On almost every patient visit, he convinced Uncle Peter to stop at the jetty at the foot of Blackfriars Lane. There, they would watch the endless array of boats plying the Thames, bringing goods and passengers to and from London. He was forever fascinated by this activity, his expansive imagination making up a story for each boat. He questioned why some boats were faster than others, even though they all shared the same wind. Curious, he thought. Uncle Peter also loved the jetty. For him, the view revealed the vibrant pulse of the City of London, with the never-ceasing movement of people and goods.

Peter enjoyed his frequent trips around London with his uncle, for they appealed to his adventurous nature. The walks were more exciting than the buggy rides, as he was able to see more and hear the people. He knew that he wasn't old enough to venture out on his own because the streets of London abounded with pickpockets, rowdies, and gangs, all a threat to adults and much more dangerous to children, who represented easy prey. He especially liked walking through the markets with his uncle, never tiring of the smells, sights, and sounds. There were rows of carcasses on display in butchers' stalls, vegetables and fruits of all variety at the green grocers' shops, and all manner of sea creatures, most still alive, at the fishmongers' booths. Pigs roamed freely, seeking food, and pigeons were abundant, provided black kites were not about. Humanity streamed through the market, including hawkers, shoppers, beggars, and the physically disabled, as well as the ever-present pickpockets. But he was with his Uncle Peter, and so he was safe.

Peter III first learned of the secret instrument on an occasion when Uncle Peter was unexpectedly summoned by a midwife. As Peter III waited outside the bedchamber with the husband and two women relatives, it became quite apparent that this woman was in great pain. Every two or three minutes she screamed, and the agonizing noises continued for over an hour. Then, suddenly, the screaming stopped and the woman, now elated and joyful, cried out "Thank you God, oh, thank you!" She repeated these words over and over, and he could hear a baby crying in the background. Although he didn't see the delivery, this experience was triumphant for him. He was only nine, and now he had become very worldly.

Peter excelled at the Merchant Tailors School. His classmates were all boys, of course. Girls did not go to school because they had so many things to learn about running a household, which was their duty at the time. Boys learned mathematics, grammar, rhetoric, Latin, and French. These subjects were easy for Peter after all of his tutoring at home. He was alert and competitive, and so he excelled as a scholar. He particularly enjoyed the company of his classmates and relished having discussions concerning science and mathematics whenever he could engage someone. Naturally, he enjoyed most the exercise periods when they went into the schoolyard and played leapfrog, shot bows and arrows, wrestled, and, on days when someone could supply them with an inflated pig's bladder, football. He was a little bigger than his classmates, and so he was always the captain. The most fun, though, was mounting the makeshift stage in the yard and giving impassioned harangues to any who would listen (Ackroyd 2000).

By the time he was ten, he had accompanied his Uncle Peter to the homes of laboring mothers many times. He was charged with carrying into the bedchamber the carved wooden box with brass handles that contained the secret instrument. Unlike the larger box that had required two bearers, this one was crafted so that one person, even one small person, could easily carry it. He was instructed to remain close to the box, no matter what transpired. He was the bulldog guarding a bone, letting no one near the box and opening it only after the bedchamber was locked. He was actually present in the room for many deliveries and he became very intrigued with the miracle of birth.

Chapter 13   Run-Ins with the College – 1602 – 1612

Peter the Younger became increasingly busy; as a result, he was called before the officers of the Barber-Surgeons Company three times for missing the required lectures, once in 1602 and twice in 1606 (Aveling 1882). More seriously, in subsequent years he was summoned by the College of Physicians on several occasions to answer charges that he had been practicing Physick, or medicine, the prerogative of the members of the Royal College of Physicians. These were humiliating experiences for Peter. He had always tried to do the correct thing, and he was embarrassed to be in conflict with his own professional organization, much more the College of Physicians.

How could so upright a man have become the subject of such accusations? The truth is that as his practice grew and his reputation spread, Peter had many requests to treat patients who needed medications. As a barber-surgeon, he knew he could not do so. Nevertheless, occasionally, he would accede to one of these requests probably out of convenience or as a favor to a friend or long-time patient. Hence, in August 1607, one Dr. Ridley, who was jealous of Peter's success, accused him of having prescribed medicine as an electuary, a paste of water and honey mixed with the medicine, to a son of Mr. Lile, and of having given pills to a girl that had caused a diarrhea lasting three days. These accusations were devastating to Peter. He knew that he had the knowledge and skill to practice Physick, but it was forbidden, so now he appeared as a scofflaw to the members of his professional society and felt disgraced.

In November 1607, another physician, Dr. Rawlins, accused him of illegal and evil practice, for he had undertaken the treatment of a certain Richard Welch, living on Thames Street and afflicted with joint disease, by means of ointments and potions, sudorifics to produce sweat, and purgatives. Peter pleaded that he had acted on the authority of his father-in-law, Dr. de Laune, a well-known physician. In actuality, he had made a bargain with the patient and had concocted the treatment in his home without the prescription of his father-in-law. He was fined five marks. Peter accepted his fate and did not try again to join the College of Physicians. His rejection only served to increase his hatred and contempt for the College, a hatred that was to grow over the years.

If Peter's problems with the College of Physicians were bad, his older brother's were much worse. In truth, he had a greater propensity to practice medicine, perhaps because he had had a longer professional association with their father, William, and because he had regularly practiced medicine himself in Southampton. It is, therefore, not surprising to find frequent complaints in the Annals of the Royal College of Physicians about Peter the Elder's failure to confine his professional activities to surgery. In December 1609, he was cited to appear before the President and the Censors of the College, accused of *"praxis medica illegitica et mala."* He did not respond, which certainly must have incurred their wrath. Cited again the same month, he again did not respond. In January 1610, he was also cited, but once more he did not show up. Then, in March 1610, he finally deigned to appear and was assessed a fine of 40 shillings, which he successfully bargained down to 20 shillings and then promptly paid.

It must be admitted that many of Peter the Elder's difficulties were the result of his own actions, but certainly some were due to envy. The officers of the College bitterly resented his associations with royalty and particularly his frequent appearances at Court. Several of the officers actually hated him, and so his persistence in practicing Physick was especially irksome to them (Aveling 1882). It was only a matter of time before worse would come from them.

"In 1612, Peter the Elder again appeared before the Censors of the College of Physicians, having been accused of practicing Physick on a Mrs. Mills in "My Lord Mayor's house." He had given her a drink to dry up moisture which he supposed came from her back; the drink he had concocted himself. It was unanimously agreed that he gave the medicine wrongly, and the practice was condemned." (Aveling 1882)

A hearing was held at the College of Physicians and the accused was present to answer questions and offer any possible explanations in his defense. But, in this setting, it must have been daunting for a mere barber-surgeon to face the dreaded Censors who were elite, university educated physicians. The Censors had experienced repeated episodes of transgressions on the part of the Chamberlen brothers. It is not hard to imagine how exasperated they were with the Chamberlens. But what would be an appropriate punishment?

The Censors held a special meeting on November 17, 1612, at the College to determine Peter's fate. He was not allowed to attend. This august body had the authority to assign punishment that could range from a reprimand to a fine or, in particularly serious cases, imprisonment. By now the officers of the College of Physicians had become angry with the incorrigible Peter the Elder and his continued, flagrant practice of medicine. They discussed the full range of punishments, but they quickly determined that the only way to deal with him was imprisonment.

Chapter 14   Newgate Prison - 1612

The rulers of London seemed obsessed with incarcerating people. They had 18 gaols in London, far more than any other city in Europe. London certainly had its share of serious criminals—murderers, thieves and arsonists—but it is notable that the jails also were full of persons whose only crimes were such offenses as bankruptcy, debt, or vagrancy.

The story of Newgate dates back to early 1200s when prisoners were confined in the gatehouse of London's 5th gate to the city. Newgate prison was used for incarcerating persons who had committed serious and minor crimes, creating a miserable environment for those whose offense was simply to be in debt. It was also the site for criminals condemned to die by hanging. The leading offences that brought about hanging were burglary (20%), forgery (17%), highway robbery (13%), murder (8.3%), theft (8.2%) and horse stealing (6.8%).

The underground dungeons for those condemned to death were notorious. The entry was through a small hatch in the ceiling. The floor contained open sewers in two corners with a stream of raw sewage connecting them. The prisoners were often shackled and chained, existing in an environment of stench and darkness. Many tales of cruelty, brutality, and violence on part of the keepers give some hint at how horrendous the conditions were. In 1537, 11 Catholic monks "were left, standing and chained to pillars, to die of starvation" (Ackroyd 2000).

In the 15th century conditions were so horrible that reformer Richard Wittington left money in his will for change. The prison was rebuilt in 1423 with three sides: the Masters side was for prisoners who could afford to pay for food, drink, and favors; the Commoners side for those unfortunate souls who had nothing with which to buy favors, occupied by debtors and felons alike, and finally, the Press Yard for prisoners of note (Ackroyd 2000). Changes occurred in the physical building and even in the way prisoners were treated but all too soon the prison slipped back into its former dismal state.

The day after the Censors' decision at the College of Medicine, two marshals dressed in official uniforms emerged from a carriage in front of Peter the Elder's home. Although he must have realized that imprisonment in the dreaded Newgate was a distinct possibility, it is likely he had not until then feared the decision of the Censors. He had many prominent and powerful friends who helped to make the possibility of imprisonment seem very remote, thus it is likely he had a strong case of denial. But such denial must have ended suddenly, when two marshals escorted him to the looming door of Newgate Prison and he was confronted with irons and shackles. If that wasn't jolting enough, surely the slamming shut of the door to his 7 by 9 foot cell was sufficient to rattle any man to the bones. The cells were dark and dank, very like a tomb. Fetid odors would have constantly reminded Peter of his dismal state. Even the rats that ambled through his cell would defy his presence.

Peter, now 52 years of age, was remarkably well knit for a man who had lived so long, still tall and strong and with all his teeth. He was focused, determined, and cautiously optimistic, which was reassuring, for as an inmate he would need all of these attributes just to survive.

Peter the Elder's plight during his incarceration was horrible, but not as bad as for those without money. Peter's only connection with the outside world would have been a jailer who would make it plain from the start that he could do favors, provided he was paid sufficiently. Being a man of wealth was Peter's single advantage in this oppressive world. For a few coins his jailer was at his service, relaying letters and messages, and supplying extra food which was generally disgusting. In spite of the bought favors, conditions were appalling.

81

Peter's first message would have been to Anne to report that he was alive and determined to get out of the prison as soon as possible. Almost certainly he would have instructed Anne not to try to visit and above all not to even think of having little Ester visit for the situation would be too shocking. Besides, he could ask his brother to make any necessary visits. His next message would have been to Peter the Younger who would surely want to visit and help him to get out of prison, as his brother hated the College for all of its arbitrary and unkind reprimands, and especially now for this major injustice to his older brother. Other parts of the message would have been to tell him that, as much as he missed Peter III, this scene could be too upsetting for a 12 year-old boy and that if Peter III were to visit, to be sure to avoid coming on a Monday, as that was the time when all prisoners condemned to death were assembled in the yard just outside the debtor's door and put in a cart to travel to the Tyburn hanging site. Whether Peter III came to Newgate is not known, but certainly Peter the Younger came to see what he could do for his unfortunate brother.

Before we learn of Peter's fate, let's fast-forward to Newgate's future. The Great Fire of 1666 burned everything in its path; even the huge Newgate complex succumbed, eradicating one of the city's notorious institutions from London's landscape. Predictably, this prison, essential to the function of London's system of criminal justice, was rebuilt on this very site just four years later where it has stood for centuries. The new prison had five sides to accommodate the various categories of criminals. Initially there were few changes to the dungeons for those condemned to hang. The other categories fared better especially those who could pay for favors. In the basement to the right of the prison entrance was a room run by an inmate where those who could afford it could buy cheap gin, day and night, called "Cock-my-Cap" and "Comfortt." Many of the prisoners drank themselves into oblivion (Ackroyd 2000). Over the years numerous attempts at improving the conditions were made and gradually true prison reform was achieved.

By 1783 the hanging in Tyburn had become such a popular social event that the transport of condemned prisoners caused traffic jams. Thus the hangings were transferred to the grounds of Newgate Prison which made accommodations for the public to witness the events from stands and provided a Newgate publication telling of the event, all for a price.

On June 3, 1902 the last prisoner was executed at Newgate symbolizing the beginning of the end. Four months later the famous prison was razed. It is ironic that Newgate, the prison that hosted cruelty, violence, and injustice, had become the new site for Old Bailey, the Central Criminal Court, or London's hall of justice.

Chapter 15   Queen Anne Intercedes

With Peter the Elder jailed, the wheels of power started to turn fast. He was a respected professional and an honest man and that demanded attention in 17th Century England. Fortunately for Peter Chamberlen, communication from his jail cell was not a problem. He was able to bring the full force of his considerable influence into play. The Lord Mayor, at his request, came to his defense. His cousin, Thomas Chamberlen, Master of the powerful Mercer's Guild, interceded on his behalf. The judges of the Kingdom made a demand on their authority and writ that he be released. But the College of Physicians could and did deny this release for the offense was of the gravest level: malpractice (Aveling 1882, page 8). The outlook seemed bleak for Peter.

Queen Anne was very upset and angered when she learned that her man-midwife, Peter Chamberlen, had been sent to jail by the College of Physicians. She immediately summoned the Archbishop of Canterbury to the Palace and told him that she was appalled that the College of Physicians had imprisoned her personal midwife. She demanded Peter Chamberlen be released from jail immediately. The Archbishop was most eager to have the opportunity to help the Queen, for he had been trying to convert her from her rumored Catholic leanings to the Anglican Church. He immediately went to work to free Peter, using his authority and most persuasive skills on the President and Censors of the Royal College. The College certainly had the authority to sentence Peter the Elder to prison, but the Archbishop, acting on behalf of the Queen, was a very compelling force. He prevailed, and shortly Peter was released from Newgate Prison, Queen Anne paying the fines.

The officers of the College of Physicians were shocked by this action. After all, their authority originated with a charter from King Henry VIII, set forth in 1518, and it was inviolate;

furthermore, Peter Chamberlen's sentence was for the worst of all offenses, malpractice. Never had one of the College's rulings been overturned, especially not a sentence to prison.

The President and Censors of the College of Physicians, realizing they had suffered an assault on their authority, immediately petitioned an audience with the Archbishop of Canterbury. The Archbishop received them promptly and cordially. He greeted each in the party individually, calling them by name and title. The Archbishop's large meeting room was surprisingly austere, considering that he was a man of such power. In addition to the Archbishop, two bishops and a scribe were in attendance.

The President announced that they were there on most serious business. The Royal College of Physicians was the oldest medical organization in England. Their founding charter from King Henry authorized them alone to determine who was eligible to be a physician, to grant or deny licenses, and to punish those who had not performed properly in this profession. They cannot have this authority undermined. Mr. Peter Chamberlen was guilty of malpractice, having demonstrated his transgressions by many acts in the past. They had to mete out appropriate punishment. If the Archbishop overturns their judgments, they simply cannot do their charge and chaos will ravage medicine in London. They demanded that the Archbishop uphold their authority and privileges. Nothing more, nothing less.

The Archbishop indicated that they were honorable, learned, and wise men who perform an invaluable service to the people of London. He explained that Mr. Peter Chamberlen, the Elder, was a unique case. He was released from Newgate, and indeed pardoned, because he was the man-midwife to the Queen. After explaining that it was a matter of the highest priority and delicacy, he assured them that he would vigorously resist any future assaults upon the privileges and authority of the College.

The President indicated that they were satisfied and took formal cognizance that the Archbishop duly recognized their authority and privileges. Peter Chamberlen's name never appeared in the Annals of the Royal College again (Aveling 1882).

* * *

After his release from Newgate Prison, Peter's first act was to request an audience with Queen Anne, and accordingly he dispatched a messenger to the Palace. The messenger returned, bearing the news that an afternoon audience would be granted in three days. Peter must have been relieved, for he needed time to collect his thoughts and purge his body of the Newgate filth.

A meeting occurred between Queen Anne and Peter the Elder. At the appointed time, Peter arrived at the Palace. Queen Anne was seated on her throne as he entered the hall. As she motioned him to step forward, he realized they were quite alone in the room save for the guards at the entrance to the chamber. Queen Anne observed him closely as he approached the throne. His heart was racing, partly because he was awed to be in the presence of royalty and partly because he was so happy to see his savior. Five paces from the throne, Peter knelt and bowed his head.

"Arise, my loyal subject. Welcome."

Peter for a moment could say nothing. Though usually a man who could master his feelings, he was so grateful for the Queen's kindness that he had to fight back tears. "My gracious Queen, I bring you my eternal gratitude and loyalty." Momentarily, he thought he would tell her how horrid the experience had been. Then, coming to his senses, he bowed his head and fell silent again.

The Queen smiled and looked down at him. "Master Chamberlen, you are an important member of this Court.

You have served your Queen well. I could not tolerate the injustice your colleagues had levied on you."

"I am overwhelmed by your kindness, your Majesty."

With that, Queen Anne removed a significant, brilliant diamond ring from her index finger and presented it to Peter. He was thunderstruck. "My Queen, you are far too generous! I am unworthy. But I humbly accept this gift and shall forever be dedicated to your service."

"Your talent and skills may be needed in the future. You are dismissed."

* * *

This ring is listed in Peter the Elder's will dated November 29, 1631, as a legacy to his granddaughter. "I give unto the said Anne Cargill my diamond ringe which I had of Queene Anne to be kept or sold for her as my Executor shall see fitt" (Aveling 1882, page 11).

Chapter 16   Training the London Midwives

What motivated the Chamberlen brothers to bring the midwives into Peter the Younger's home for education and training? It seems clear that the Chamberlen family had a strong dedication to teaching. William had educated his sons in the art of healing and they easily passed the barber surgeon's exam which indicated a high level of proficiency as trained practitioners. Their childbirth experiences with the midwives provided evidence to them that the midwives sorely needed education. To that end, they started monthly sessions at Peter the Younger's home. Their motivation appears to be altruistic. The question of organizing and incorporating the midwives is less clear. Having a cadre of well-trained midwives to work with would clearly improve the outcome of deliveries saving many babies and mothers. It also had an element of financial gain for the Chamberlens for it assured that these midwives would call them and only them for delivery assistance. Generally, people seek "pure motives" to explain situations, to categorize them into good or evil. However, in real life I believe mixed motives are more common. Surely the babies and the mothers were better off due to the Chamberlens' efforts and to date no one else had stepped forward to provide effective education for the midwives.

For some time the Chamberlen brothers had been appalled by the lack of training of the midwives in and about London. On balance many of the midwives practiced to the best of their ability. Yet, in this setting of limited education and training bad results were common. One midwife had delivered a baby's head, but when the rest of the baby would not deliver, she had tugged so forcefully that the head was torn from the body. Another had watched an obstructed labor for three days, until the baby died, but had never called for their aid; on the fourth day the mother died as well. Countless other horror stories could be related, but they are so gruesome and sorrowful that I shall refrain.

They had a technique that could produce a healthy baby in obstructed labors, but if the midwives didn't call them until the baby was dead or nearly so, it was to no avail. They were determined to educate the midwives, but most of them were illiterate. There were no books on midwifery anyway. They attempted to find some way to teach these women how to recognize problems early and then call for help. They decided to assemble the ones who wanted to learn and better themselves and teach them.

In February 1614 the two brothers, after many discussions and much planning, started training midwives in Peter the Younger's home. They began by holding monthly meetings with the best of the London midwives who had been calling them for assistance with difficult births. The evenings included a lecture given by the brothers, a discussion led by both, and finally a presentation telling of a particularly difficult delivery by a midwife. The midwives were taught how to identify potential problems such as obstructed labor, abnormal presentation of the baby, and hemorrhage—"flooding," as they called it.

The favorite event of the evening was always a special dinner prepared in the Chamberlens' kitchen under the exquisite guidance of Sarah. This meal often included such elegant delicacies as capon, swan, and venison, accompanied by the best of wines. The wine was always a particular treat, for Peter loved wine and always managed to have a special selection for the occasion. After the class, all sat around the large dining room table, starting each meal with grace and ending with warm compliments to Sarah. There was one strict rule for these dinners; no one was allowed to talk about deliveries at Sarah's table. That was no hardship, for the midwives could always be prompted to talk and boast about their children.

Under the direction of the Chamberlen brothers, the midwives' skills and knowledge grew, as did their gratitude and loyalty to their mentors. This special group of women felt fortunate to belong to this association. They knew that they could send for the Chamberlens whenever they needed them and that they would always get reliable help. Furthermore, they knew that for obstructed labors and complications, the Chamberlens had a secret instrument that could produce a live baby, while other midwives were using barber-surgeons who would resort to the hook or some other horribly destructive device. They were thankful to the Chamberlens for helping them in emergencies, but also for the knowledge they had imparted. And to be sure they felt considerable and well-earned pride in their new skills.

Gradually and carefully, the cadre accepted new members who were eager to learn and who could be trusted in their loyalty to the group and to the Chamberlens. The standards for acceptance were rigorous and some were rejected if they were considered uneducable by the Chamberlens, who were determined to recruit only the best in London.

Certainly not all the midwives of London wanted to join the company. Some remained fiercely independent and objected strongly to any association with barber-surgeons. Small wonder that the midwives not associated with their group became increasingly resentful of the training sessions and the Chamberlens themselves. In a profession that had been the sole province of women for many centuries, such feelings could be contained only so long.

Chapter 17   The Petition

After the Chamberlen brothers had been training midwives successfully for several years, they decided it finally was time for a formal petition organizing and incorporating the midwives of London. They knew the simplest route would be to present a proposal to the College of Physicians, but by this time Peter the Younger's hatred and mistrust of the College had become so fierce that he refused even to consider dealing with them. Instead, he convinced his brother to go to their friend King James with the petition.

Agreeing that the College would likely oppose any enterprise they might undertake, Peter requested and was granted an audience with King James.

* * *

As the King gave him leave to speak, he came directly to the point. "Your Majesty, the state of midwifery in London is deplorable. In fact, the Archbishop provides no standards for licensing and no system for educating the midwives who attend our women. Moreover, there is virtually no supervision. Consequently, countless mothers and babies die unnecessarily, and many of the babies that survive are maimed for life. It is a great shame and a great loss for England."

The King listened attentively. "I have no doubt that many of the things you say are true, Master Chamberlen. And what would you propose to amend them?"

"Our petition states, Sire, that some system may be settled by the state, being Yourself, for the instruction and civil government of the midwives." Peter went on to present a convincing argument that childbirth care in London would improve immeasurably if only he and his brother could be put in charge of educating midwives and of helping with deliveries in difficult cases.

"Besides," he concluded, "we have a special instrument. Its use could save the lives of many mothers and babies every year."

* * *

King James was so impressed with this proposal from his trusted subject that he needed no more convincing. He would give the brothers the support they sought if they would make a formal proposal.

Following Peter the Elder's appearance before the King, the brothers submitted a "humble petition of the midwives in and about the City of London... that the said midwives be incorporated and made a society" (Dunn 1999). The petition was addressed to King James and Sir Francis Bacon, a member of the Privy Council. Of course the King was already aware of the proposal and in favor of supporting the Chamberlens, and his sentiments were well known in Court. The Privy Council referred the petition to the College of Physicians for consideration, which was unfortunate for the Chamberlens, because the College never considered favorably anything these barber-surgeons did.

The midwives at this time were either employed by the Bishop or were independent practitioners. There must have been some meetings of midwives to object to the Chamberlens' scheme, for after all, it was their livelihood that was at stake. Of course, they were not organized as a guild or professional society and they had little voice in their fate and probably little entré to information on what was occurring. No information could be found about any meetings of midwives to oppose the Chamberlens' initiative. At this juncture the only organization of midwives was the one created by and loyal to the Chamberlens. What a difference two decades would make.

Chapter 18   Showdown

The Chamberlens penned a formal petition in detail and delivered it to King James. The King studied the petition and referred it to his counselors, who in turn had referred it to the College of Physicians.

Can you imagine the posture of the College of Physicians upon receiving a proposal from King James for the Chamberlens to incorporate all of the midwives of London? The Chamberlen brothers had been cited, fined and punished many times for offenses, mainly practicing Physick, judged by them to be a criminal act. Just four years earlier they had sentenced Peter the Elder to Newgate Prison for practicing Physick. When the Archbishop, at the behest of the Queen, had Peter the Elder released from prison, despite his direct encroachment on the College's professional territory, it did major damage to their authority. This petition was an emotional and contentious matter for the College and drew much attention in London.

On January 24, 1616, the College of Physicians met to consider the incorporation of midwives. After concerned discussion, the College officials decided the Censors should weigh the matter and commit their opinions to writing. In addition, they decreed that the President should consult with Doctors Mountford, Lister, Palmer, and Argent, considered among the most learned and wisest in the profession, and then report their conclusions to the College (Aveling 1882).

The College convened again on February 21, 1616, at which time the opinions of the members were brought forward and discussed in Peter the Younger's presence and directly recorded. Below is the hearing as I imagine it.

* * *

Peter was asked whether he thought his judgments in cases of difficult labor would be more likely to be correct than the judgments of any member of the College.

"My answer, my Lord, after many years' experience, is that I and my brother and none others excel in these subjects."

"Is that not an overly strong statement, Mr. Chamberlen?"

"I only can report what I know to be true."

"We shall deliberate and present a report shortly; this hearing is closed."

* * *

Some two weeks later, the President of the College of Physicians issued a report to the Lords of the Privy Council, which read in part as follows:

"The College of Physicians do hold it very convenient that a Reformation were had of the abuses as are mentioned in the petition. And also some means used for the bettering of the skill of the Midwives (who for the most part are very ignorant). Nevertheless they think it neither necessary nor convenient that they should be made a corporation to govern within themselves, a thing not exampled in any Commonwealth.

The College also maketh offer to depute such grave and learned men as shall always be ready to resolve all their doubts and instruct them in what they desire concerning midwifery and once or twice in the years to make private dissections and Anatomies to the use of their whole Company."

(Aveling 1882)

Finally, the College, with a wariness of ecclesiastical authority born of bitter experience, suggested mildly that the midwives "before they be admitted by the Bishop or his

Chancellor be first examined and approved by the President of the College of Physicians and two or three of the gravest of that Society such as the President shall nominate."

This seems to be very self-serving on the part of the College of Physicians, but, they did indeed exercise authority over medical practice in all of London. The learned men of the College were medical and not surgical, and they likely were deficient in knowledge of the generative anatomy. Nonetheless, had the College somehow become involved in evaluating the suitability of midwifery candidates it would have changed the history of midwifery. With the College's capacity for organization and function and their enormous resource of educated physicians, they would have managed to develop appropriate evaluation techniques, aiding the Bishop to make proper selections

The College's ruling was a major setback for the Chamberlen brothers. Had they worked so hard to raise the standards of midwifery only to have their efforts repudiated by the College of Physicians at last? The fate of their entire enterprise was now in jeopardy. To add insult to injury, the authorities demeaned Peter the Younger by referring to him thus in the College records:

> "To Peter Chamberlen, the Younger, who was impudently advocating the cause of these women, the question was put, whether, if any difficulty in a case of labour were propounded to any member of the College he would not answer and judge more correctly than any obstetric surgeon whatever, in spite of his boast that he and his brother, and none others, excelled in these subjects." (Aveling 1882)

This putdown must have caused the Chamberlens great disconsolation and humiliation. Though they were both spirited men who ordinarily would never give up and admit defeat, the tide of events seemed to have turned against them. To make matters worse, later in 1616, Queen Anne died tragically after a long bout with joint pain and massive

95

swelling in her lower extremities. Peter the Elder was greatly saddened by her passing. The Queen had been not only a friend but also a very influential supporter. The Chamberlen brothers had lost the pillar of their political advantage.

At a meeting on June 3, 1617, a letter from the College to the Lords of the Council relating to the position of the midwives was read aloud and the Registrar was ordered to make an accurate copy. In short, it rejected the Chamberlen proposal. Licensing of midwives would continue to be left in the hands of the Bishops of the Church of England.

This was a tragic decision since the level of midwifery practiced in England was deplorable, and far behind most of the European countries, which almost uniformly had municipal regulation and supervision of the midwives by physicians. Had they been permitted to incorporate, the Chamberlens would have brought education and training standards to the midwives. Needless losses of babies and mothers could have been avoided. But this was not to be at this time, and the women and children of England were the losers.

Chapter 19   Dr. Peter's Education

Peter III had excelled in his studies at the Merchant Tailors' School, and it was now time for him to go to university. His father and Uncle Peter had already decided it would be Cambridge rather than Oxford because of its reputation for excellence in science. This great university had been established in 1209 by a group of Oxford scholars who wanted to escape the frequent "town-gown riots." Its first college, Peterhouse, was founded in 1284 by the Bishop of Ely of the Benedictine order. Since then, many other colleges had sprung up on the sprawling site by the banks of the Cam River, as the university gradually came to dominate the tiny farming and trade town. In 1584, Emmanuel College was built on the site of a Dominican house, and it became the favorite of Puritans and Calvinists. Since most of the other colleges were devoted to producing lawyers and future pastors of the Anglican churches throughout England, the choice of Emmanuel seemed ideal for Peter III both because he was a Calvinist and because of his interest in science.

On April 25, 1615, at age 14, he matriculated at Emmanuel College with the intention of studying science and medicine. It should not be a surprise that Peter was accompanied by both his father and Uncle Peter on his first journey there, for by now their drive for him to become a physician, in my judgment, qualified as an obsession. They seemed committed to delivering him personally into the guardianship of his Cambridge don, though of course, there was no need for them to do so. It wasn't as if Peter would bolt on the way to Cambridge and forego the opportunity to acquire a university education. On the contrary, Peter thrived on learning. He had been brought up with frequent tutoring in the art of medicine by his father and Uncle Peter, not to mention his maternal Grandfather, William de Laune. By his own accounts, they taught him Chyrurgical (surgical) operations, Galenical methods of extracting constituents of plants, and Chemical Science. Peter had been schooled in Latin, Greek, German, and certainly his ancestral language, French. He adored mathematics and science and wanted very much to go to Cambridge, although he must have had qualms that he might be a bit too young to start at that time.

Perhaps there was another reason why both his father and Uncle Peter accompanied him. These men had distinguished careers by this time, yet Peter the Elder was an immigrant and Peter the Younger was born of immigrant parents and neither had attended university. In their profession as barber-surgeons, they would have been reminded daily by their superiors, the physicians, that they lacked a university education. Surely, these men must have experienced a wide gamut of emotions on this trip, as Peter III was the first member of their family to enroll in a university.

Fascinated by Peter's academic accomplishments, I visited Cambridge to experience firsthand the site of his education. While Emmanuel College certainly has had many additions and changes since Peter's matriculation in 1615, there are many features that are little changed, such as the venerable old dining hall, the old library and some of the dormitories. Most impressive was the book of matriculation kept in the new library, in which Peter's signature can be viewed. This is quite remarkable, for a sample of his handwriting was eminently legible compared to the signatures of many of my present day medical colleagues. More importantly, it is stylish, deliberate, and clearly the handwriting of someone proud of who he is at age 14.

Early on the morning of their departure, Uncle Peter arrived to accompany young Peter on his journey. Peter and his father bid goodbye to Sarah while the groom loaded their saddlebags onto their horses. Sarah brought them two baskets of food and drink for their trip. Getting out of London at this hour was easy, exiting through Bishopsgate.

Ahead lay a 60-mile journey by way of the London-Cambridge road, which was relatively passable by the standards of English country roads in those days. The custom was for each tollhouse to maintain the road that passed through its confines. Many parts of the road, however, ran through wild, deserted trails as the route followed the old Roman road. This portion of the trip could be jolting and slow. In other instances, the road was merely a track-way, becoming almost impassable on rainy days.

The trip took fifteen hours in all. Since traveling at night on dark roads would invite attacks by highwaymen and unemployed ex-soldiers, midway they stayed overnight at a

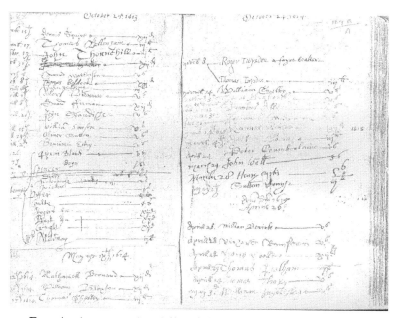

Peter's signature (middle of the right page), Emmanuel College matriculation – 1615

(Courtesy of Emmanuel College at Cambridge)

posthouse. They awoke with the dawn, headed their horses to Cambridge, and traveled several hours before encountering rolling hills, a signal that they were nearing their destination. As they approached the town, they passed rows of old wooden warehouses, and then crossed over the pretty little Cam River on a rickety bridge. The yellow brick buildings of the town were not very attractive, but the colleges beyond were handsome with their fine stonework and stately arches. Most were situated on the banks of the Cam with gardens stretching down to the water's edge. The quadrangles bustled with people, so they passed barely noticed. They toured the colleges for hours before meeting Peter's Emmanuel College don, a junior fellow of the college who would be responsible for Peter's education at Cambridge. He was tall, the folds of his academic robe hanging straight downward from his broad shoulders. He radiated warmth, with his smile and upturned palms welcoming them as they entered. His lodgings consisted of a sitting room with two walls of books and a third occupied by a large fireplace. To the rear of the room was the door to his small sleeping quarters.

The don explained that as first to arrive, Peter would have his choice of beds. His classmates would arrive the next day. Two were "pizars" so they would have to do chores — nothing too rigorous, but nonetheless a responsibility they must fulfill. Peter was a "pension ordinary," so he was exempt from chores at Emmanuel. His curriculum would prepare him for science and medicine. The don asked Peter's father and Uncle Peter about their profession and seemed genuinely interested in what they had to say. Because of his interest in science, the don had many questions for them. Then he explained how Peter's education would proceed at Cambridge. They listened carefully as he described Peter's impending metamorphosis into an independent scholar. Each evening, Peter would meet with him for discussion and discourse. He would receive comments and directions and then proceed to study on his own until their meeting the next evening. To Peter's surprise, he gave him a weighty tome to read for their evening meeting the next day. Peter's time with his father and Uncle Peter ended with a light dinner at an inn. They said their farewells, and then the two men departed for London, hoping to reach a post-house before dark.

The room where Peter would dwell was rudimentary in its appointments but quite satisfactory. It was large, containing three beds, a table, chairs, and a fireplace. As he was the first to arrive, he chose the bed under the window and the corner bookcase. His first act probably was to exchange his lumpy palliasse for a less lumpy one from one of the other beds. His luggage had come by horse wagon and had been piled neatly in a corner.

The large room was adjacent to the don's apartment. To the rear of this room was a tiny alcove containing a cot and a bench. This was the province of the gyp, the man responsible for the general upkeep of their rooms and the stoking of the fire. His don explained that the gyp would make porridge for them in the morning, but that for other meals, they must hike to the dining hall where they would be served at long tables. At the end of the dining hall, was "the high table," a raised platform where the professors and dons ate.

One of Peter's classmates, as son of a nobleman, was a "fellow commoner." As such his circumstances were considerably more comfortable than Peter's. He merited his own room and ate at the high table with the dons. His father had furnished him with his own valet, tailor, and tennis master, all living in quarters nearby in Cambridge. After one week, his valet replaced his palliasse with a mattress. So, of course, there were different classes of students, each with different privileges, but this was a well-accepted tradition.

Emmanuel College boasted a real tennis court. It was the perfect year-round game, played indoors and in any weather. In good weather they hired a punt for a relaxing time on the Cam, or went to "the backs" of King's College for a hike and picnic in the meadows.

Emmanuel College Chapel (Loggan 1675)

Peter enjoyed his studies at Cambridge immensely. They explored many areas of science, and he was promptly introduced to Chirurgery (surgery). He liked anatomy and dissection, but was disappointed that they were working mainly on animals rather than humans. Sometimes his gusto for anatomy got a little out of hand, as when he brought his newly appropriated sand shark back to his room for dissection, hiding it under his bed for two days, bringing it out only when no roommates were around. At the end of 24 hours, his roommates had surmised that something horribly foul had occurred in the room. The gyp was directed to search for a dead rodent. That was the day they had the new rule barring anatomy dissections in their quarters.

Cambridge was close enough to London to allow Peter the luxury of an occasional visit. One of his trips home was to celebrate Uncle Gideon's triumph in being appointed as the first President of the Apothecaries. The Apothecaries had been part of the Grocer's Guild, founded in 1345. In 1617,

King James recognized their right to exist as a separate body, establishing by royal decree "The Worshipful Society of Apothecaries." Their charter stated that they had the right to "have, purchase, retain, and appoint a certain Hall, or Counsel-House" in the city. As yet, the Society did not have sufficient funds to buy a hall, but they were able to mount an elegant ceremony to install the officers. Peter had always been very close to Uncle Gideon, who looked much like his mother and had her warm and upright qualities, so he was delighted to be included in the celebration.

Despite completing and excelling in his studies at Cambridge, he realized after two years that he needed more education in certain subjects and that he might not be able to acquire it there. He had learned much but had little experience in physiology and almost none in human anatomy. Having heard of the great universities on the Continent, he was determined to take advantage of them. Of course, his father approved anything he asked for in the name of receiving a medical education. And so, at age 16, confident in his future and ever in pursuit of greater knowledge, he embarked for Heidelberg, Germany.

For the study of physiology, the great University of Heidelberg was his best choice. It had been established in 1385 as a Roman Catholic University, with faculties for study in philosophy, religion, jurisprudence, and medicine. In 1563, however, Heidelberg became a Calvinist institution, reorganized under the new catechism. In light of that, it was not difficult to convince his father, or Uncle Peter, that this was the right place for him.

At Heidelberg, he participated in public exercises in anatomy and physiology. As a boy, he had been tutored in German, so he had no difficulty using the Teutonic tongue as the main language for his studies. In turn, his professors enjoyed showing that they understood English and took every opportunity to answer his questions in English. After evening studies, they commonly ate dinner in bierhausen along the Neckar River. As at Cambridge, he proceeded well in his studies and thoroughly enjoyed university life. The physiology courses at Heidelberg were excellent, but the anatomy courses were only slightly better than those at Cambridge, with little attention paid to human structures. Determined to learn more, he decided after a year to move to the University of Padua, renowned as the leading center in the world for the study of anatomy. Once again, his father approved.

Ever the eager student, he found the atmosphere at the University of Padua even more exhilarating than that of either Cambridge or Heidelberg. Padua, a beautiful ancient city then under the rule of the Venetians, was famous for its botanical gardens. He had the good luck to be attending at a time of enormous transformation in the science of medicine. The history leading up to these changes fascinated Peter, and he strove to find out all he could about it.

During the Second Century CE, there lived a man named Galen, who was to have a profound influence on medicine in Europe for 13 centuries. Galen was born in Greece in 130. When he was 15 years of age, his father was visited in a dream by Aesculapius, the Greek god of physicians, who bade him have his son study the healing arts. Galen received this calling gladly. He was curious by nature and set out to learn all he could about the great physicians, even though many had lived 500 years earlier. He studied the works of Hippocrates and Diocles, as well as those of Erasistratus, a scholar of organs, and Herophilus, who had described the four humors — yellow bile, phlegm, blood, and black bile — that governed the bodily health of humans. Herophilus explained that the effects of these humors derived from their correspondence to the four elements that make up all matter — fire, water, air, and earth. Another popular theory in Galen's time was that of the *pneuma*, a sort of spirit that was thought to float through the body passages and perform various functions, as needed. Galen, a codifier and textbook

104

writer, gleaned all of the concepts that made sense to him and recorded them, amassing a huge body of medical knowledge.

Galen was a man of strong character, egotistical and dogmatic, so forceful and learned that his teachings were readily accepted by all. After a time, he moved to Rome and was immediately acclaimed as a revered medical authority, treating many of the ruling class. He studied the functions of the heart and the makeup of the brain, and knew the difference between motor and sensory nerves.

Galen set down his theories of medicine at the time of the spreading of the Christian religion, as people accepted one God and rejected the multiple deities of the pagans. Although Galen was a monotheist, he was neither Christian nor Jew. His beliefs, however, were close enough to those of the Christians for the Church to espouse his medical dicta. In time, his writings became gospel, so that one dared not contradict them any more than one would contradict the teachings of the Church Fathers themselves.

By the 1500s, most of the great universities of Europe still strictly adhered to the Galen school, and the University of Padua was no exception. It was usual during a dissection for the teacher to sit upon a high stool with a copy of Galen in one hand and a pointer in the other while he directed two students to do the actual work. It was unfortunate that sometimes what was being read from the textbook did not agree with what was revealed by the dissection.

In more recent years, the University of Padua had been dramatically influenced by an anatomist named Vesalius, a Brussels-born genius who was willing to challenge the principles of Galen, or anyone else for that matter. Vesalius became the Paduan Professor of Anatomy at age 23, and he insisted on doing his own dissections during his demonstrations. He frequently had 500 students from all over Europe attending his lectures and was promptly enlisted to teach at the Universities of Pisa and Bologna as well. Padua had now become the preeminent medical university of Europe.

In 1538, one year after his arrival at Padua, Vesalius published *Tabulae Sex*, six anatomical studies that were so clear and accurate they immediately became known throughout Europe. In fact, they were in such demand that they were quickly plagiarized. By age 24 Vesalius was firmly established as the prime authority on anatomy. By age 28, he had published his third book, *Fabrica*, which corrected many of Galen's, and even his own, errors. Dislodging precepts that had held sway for more than 1,300 years was not to be accomplished so easily however. Before long, critics who still blindly embraced Galen rose up against Vesalius and forced him out of his professorship. Discouraged, he returned to Brussels in a sorry state and destroyed his books. It was a sad ending for so brilliant a teacher, but ultimately he must have taken some pleasure in the fact that the next two Professors of Anatomy at Padua, traditionally elected by the students, were his pupils.

Steeped in the history of discovery and tradition, the University of Padua was an exciting environment for learning, as it was always on the cusp of new scientific advancements. Medical knowledge was expanding rapidly, creating new frontiers, and anatomic discoveries occurred regularly. Most stimulating for Peter were the anatomy demonstrations. As a student, he was allowed to stand next to the cadaver and, on many occasions, after being somewhat assertive, he was actually allowed to perform the dissections. How different from his experience at Cambridge, where most of his anatomy lessons employed pigs, cats, and even fish!

Peter's studies in anatomy at Padua were conducted under Professor Pederico Forsea, a distinguished member of a faculty that included the leading scientists in the world. Again, Peter's facility with languages helped him in this new setting. His hunger to learn more never slackened in this wonderful academic environment. Peter read, dissected, discussed, and grew in knowledge. But not all of the learning took place in the laboratories and libraries. After all, this region was known the world over for its reverence for food and wine, so their academic sessions often spilled into the restaurants and taverns where they discussed and debated new discoveries and old theories. Since they often had come directly from the dissecting room, they did bear a characteristic pungent odor, so it is not surprising that nearby tables promptly cleared out. During these sessions, Professor Forsea often asked provocative questions to see who would rise to his bait. Peter loved these times, but they passed all too quickly. After two years of study, at age 18, he earned the degree of Doctor of Medicine from the prestigious University of Padua and returned to London to take his place in medical practice.

In 1620, Peter was off to Oxford to incorporate that degree and, after an examination, was accorded a degree in medicine from that great institution as well. Now armed with two diplomas in medicine, and having enormous energy, he was confident and enthusiastic about his future. Nevertheless, he still had a nagging desire to add a third degree, from Cambridge.

Chapter 20   More Run-Ins: the Final Straw

While Peter III was collecting university degrees, his father was having his ups and downs. In May 1615, the College of Physicians again summoned Peter the Younger to answer charges against his practice. Though he was always honest, modest, and upright, he was no match for the organized "justice" of the College censors in these matters. In this instance, they claimed he did not know the difference in normal pulse and called it palpitation. He admitted that if he were in ignorance of the pulse, he would have been unworthy of the profession he practiced. In addition, he was charged with practicing Physick unlawfully on a Mr. Tullie, as well as on the maidservant of a certain carpenter, but as his physician accuser did not appear, according to the rule, his case was dismissed. Though he counted himself fortunate to have escaped this time without being fined or imprisoned as his brother had been, his hatred for the College grew (Aveling 1882).

In June, 1620, he was again called before the College of Physicians because he had ordered the pulp of colocynth for a sick man who had been prescribed a clyster, an enema with a syringe, by Dr. Argent and Dr. Golston then been "given over and left by them." Dr. Argent and Dr. Golston were members of the College in good standing. In fact, this was the Dr. Argent who was President of the College from 1625 to 1633 and to whom Dr. William Harvey in 1628 dedicated his famous book on the circulation of the blood (Aveling 1882, page 24-25). It was indeed the practice of these two physicians to order an enema for a patient and then discharge him from their care.

At his hearing, Peter the Younger defended himself thus: "It seemed to me a cruel thing not to succor a sick man." To explain his action, he quoted the *Practica Medica* by Massaria on the indication for colocynth, but the Censors nonetheless decided that he had prescribed it wrongly. They also accused him of other instances of "evil practice in the case of puerperal women" (women with infections form childbirth). The prospects looked dismal for Peter the Younger, but he had a trump card—a letter in his favor from his cousin, Lord Thomas Chamberlen, head of the powerful Mercers Guild. Upon producing the letter, the Censors had no choice but to discharge him "for the present," stating, "consider that you are very fortunate, because we can see no reason why you should not be sentenced to jail. You shall not practice medicine anymore or the consequences will be dire."

They had just stated that he should be sentenced to jail. He still had nightmares from his horrible visits eight years earlier to Newgate Prison to see his brother. He had witnessed his brother suffer enormous injustice at the hands of the College of Physicians. Now he was threatened with the same fate. Peter the Younger was duly admonished, but upon hearing the word "jail," he must have become enraged. How could these high and mighty fools sit there in the splendor of their office and even imagine sending a just and honorable practitioner to jail? Fortunately, at that moment, he was unable to respond and attack them verbally, for his rage robbed him of his speech. He stayed in his seat until the last of the Censors left the room. His hatred for the College was more intense than ever.

A bright moment for Peter the Younger and his family came in January, 1620, when Sarah, became a citizen of England. They celebrated the event cheerfully and shared many hours talking about her denization. In spite of the rich French heritage Sarah had endowed them with over the years, they were happy that she had chosen to become a citizen of England. She never forgot that England had provided a haven from the terrible religious persecution threatening the de Laune family in France.

By contrast, in 1620, a small group of religious separatists set sail for the New World to escape the religious persecution they felt they were suffering in England. They had their origins in Scrooby, a village in Nottinghamshire in the East Midlands. These Puritans believed that the only way they could practice their religion properly was to separate themselves from the Church of England in both theology and distance. They had first moved in 1609 to Leiden, in the religiously tolerant Netherlands. Feeling themselves constrained even there, they returned to England ten years later and contracted with a group of English merchants to establish a colony in Virginia in the New World. After recruiting more colonists to swell their numbers, they finally embarked in September 1620. Their first ship, the Mayflower, endured a difficult three-month crossing but finally arrived far north of their destination at the tip of Cape Cod, in the colony we now call Massachusetts. Finding no timbers there to build homes, they moved on to a more suitable site on the mainland coast. A second ship, the Fortune, arrived the following year. With rugged determination, the settlers set up the Plymouth Rock Colony, braving severe winters, disease, and near starvation.

Though Peter the Younger admired the courage of these separatists, he did not hold much in common with their philosophy. He was so busy that he did not pay them much mind. They did not seem to be happy anywhere, yet they had never been persecuted as the Huguenots were in France. His forebears had come to England to escape constant harassment and violence, and they had enjoyed reasonable religious freedom and tolerance in their adopted country. Perhaps it was not so easy here for the Jews and the Catholics, but a man has to be thankful for what he has.

In spite of his appreciation of religious freedom, Peter's situation with the Royal College was not to get any better. In 1621, the College of Physicians accused Peter the Younger of treating Morbus Gallicus (syphilis) by means of purging and fasting. Though he was constrained to confess to this transgression, Peter the Younger felt quite certain that he had done no harm, since he had employed this remedy successfully in his practice in Southampton. As before, he was embarrassed and humiliated to receive yet another reprimand from the College, though again he was fortunate to escape a jail sentence.

He was summoned before the College once more in July of that year and admonished not to practice medicine, after which he was discharged. Peter the Younger resolved to avoid any further confrontations with the Royal College, for now he had a more important goal: his son's becoming a member of the College.

Chapter 21   Upward Climb

In 1620, Dr. Peter petitioned Cambridge University to incorporate his medical degree. This was a system whereby the two English universities recognized qualified degrees from schools on the Continent. Though his degree from the University of Padua was deemed satisfactory, he was required to sit for three further examinations before being awarded one from Cambridge. He had no difficulty passing them, of course, and so finally achieved his goal of earning degrees from three of the greatest medical Universities. At an impressive ceremony of great solemnity, he felt awed as the Chancellor presented him with the crimson robe signifying his doctorate. He suspected his cheeks were as red as the robe: "I …. wore my scarlet (robe) under the worthy Professor of Oxford Doctour Clayton and the next year under the Doctour of the Chair in Cambridge. I confess, my Degree seemed big unto myself, and the pointing of the finger dyed my Cheeks with the reflection of the Robes. Yet I was led into Practice which God blest with Gifts of Healin" (Chamberlen 1647).

Now armed with three degrees, on January 11, 1621 Dr. Peter first appeared at the College of Physicians as a candidate for examination. The officials conducting the interview saw that there was a certification appended to his application stating that he had received a medical degree from the prestigious University of Padua after studying under the famous Professor Roderic Fonsea. They also examined his credentials from Oxford and Cambridge before accepting his application. He returned to the College office on February 8, 1621, was examined by the Censors, and was given to understand that he had passed successfully. Naturally, he had every reason to be optimistic. Several weeks later, however, he was summoned to the College and received the first indication of a brewing problem as he was examined yet another time but this time the questions and comments included some references to his flamboyant dress and his father's and his uncle's experience with the College. Following his examination on March 22, 1621 he was told he had failed and to wait and try again "with good expectation of success." He was more than disappointed; he was devastated, and, of course, so would be his father and Uncle Peter. In a state of shock, Dr. Peter returned home to face his father.

* * *

As the oldest son and student of Peter the Younger, Peter had a special relationship with his father. Returning home to face him after rejection by the College must have been very painful. Blackfriars Lane was a short, narrow passage winding downhill from Ludgate to Queen's Street, which paralleled the Thames. The timbered houses lining the lane rose up three stories, with each story projecting inward to provide shelter from the rain, making it appear that they would kiss in the center of the lane. The lane's narrowness and curves made it difficult to navigate, providing some refuge from the coach traffic that was increasingly choking the London streets.

The day was not unusual for January, the smell wafting from the Thames cesspool, at high tide, being tolerable and somewhat reminiscent of the sea. Come low tide, the ambience changed, for added to the stench of garbage and human waste was the odor of river muck and exposed sea life on the sloping edges of the river bed. The latter was now the case, and, to complete the picture, the heavy fog rolling up Blackfriars Lane seemed to flood into the narrow passageway as if seeking to escape somewhere uphill.

Peter was returning from his admission interview at the College of Physicians. As the coachman turned down the lane, Peter heard the familiar clattering of the iron wheel rims and horses' hooves on the cobblestones beneath them, followed by a squeal as the coachman gently set the brakes to ease their descent. Peter's body knew every cobble on that lane, and returning home always brought pleasure to his soul—but not today.

The coachman reined the horses to an abrupt halt. Peter opened the door and alit from the coach, taking care not to topple his plumed hat. Walking directly to the front stoop, Peter rapped impatiently on the heavy oak door. Nodding a greeting to Liddy, the maid, he brushed by her and went directly to the salon.

As he entered, he was irresistibly drawn to his father's armchair and settled into it with a sense of relief. It was a huge chair with prominent wings, covered in grainy brown leather. Overstuffed with horsehair and padding, it was comfortable and felt secure. It always provided a sense of serenity, a sure remedy for any turmoil that had occurred in the outside world. His brothers and sisters likewise enjoyed their turns in this haven, though never when Father was at home.

After adding a chunk of coal to the fire and determinedly stoking it, he turned and sat before the flames. "This room is freezing," he thought. "I must add more coal. Where in the world is Father when I need him? Those obnoxious bastards! Those arrogant ignoramuses!" He was annoyed that he had been reduced to talking to himself, but he was so distraught that he couldn't help it. He shifted in the chair, trying to get comfortable and relax. But the cocoon was not working this time. He simply could not drive the College admission interview from of his mind.

Liddy had followed him into the salon. A wisp of a person, she stood with her dark hair showing beneath her bonnet, her sad eyes belying a pleasing, melodic voice that always ended on an upward inflection.

"Pardon me, m'lord, but your father is at the Magistrate's. 'Ee 'ad a tussle with an 'ouse-breaker last night, and your father got the better of 'im. The bloke was

114

trying to crawl through the upstairs window when your father whacked him over the 'ead with a chamber pot. I am afraid it will be a while before your father returns. Can I fetch you a glass of cider or ale, m'lord?"

"No thank you, Liddy, just some quiet so I can collect my thoughts."

"As you wish, m'lord."

He surveyed the salon. It was a grand room, paneled with polished oak and with two large windows catching the late morning sun, as it cast strong rectangular patterns on the carpet. Two eight-candle chandeliers lit the room in the evenings. Tapestries adorned two of the walls, and several chests stood like sentries guarding the room. The large stone hearth loomed on the Thames side of the salon. The chairs clustered around the hearth reminded him of the countless times his family had joined together to share the warmth of the fire and hear tales of deliveries by Father. He always sat to the right of the hearth, and Mother to the left. As children, they occupied chairs or stools in a semicircle in front of the soot-blackened stone of the hearth. Each year or two, the semicircle grew as they added to our family. He remembered Mother always nursing a child or tending a rocking-cradle at her side. In this very room, his family and friends waited the night he was born, or so he was told.

The huge fireplace had room for many logs, but Father preferred burning large chunks of coal, for they lasted longer and gave off even heat. The hearth had a heavy iron arm that held a kettle for those special occasions when they enjoyed warm wine drinks together as a family. They had celebrated birthdays and many an Easter and Christmas in this room, all associated with joy and imbued with a feeling of family love and security.

Peter thought about the crisp autumn days he had spent in this room, days alternately clear, with chilling breezes, or fog-shrouded and still. On such days, they always had a fire burning in the evening. He also cherished memories of cold winter days, when the semicircle grew tighter around the hearth as they huddled for warmth. The closeness of their family seemed to manifest itself best in winter.

Peter recalled when the Thames had frozen over in January 1608. The whole family, except the baby, had skidded, slipped, and coasted down to Blackfriars jetty, where they ventured out onto the vast expanse of the frozen Thames. As far up and down the river as they could see, people were enjoying this extraordinary winter phenomenon. Merchants had moved stalls along the sides of the river to take advantage of this opportunity; there were fruit sellers, victuallers, shoe makers, and even a barber's tent. What a treat! They sledded, skated, threw snowballs, and built a snow castle, all in one afternoon. The castle glistened tall and white, as they stood proudly and admired their creation.

They were, of course, impervious to the cold, all bundled up in knitwear that their mother had crafted for them. As dusk approached, they ended this great family adventure and, holding hands, retreated to their haven on the hill.

That night, the semicircle was even smaller as they nestled nearer the hearth. The fire sputtered, crackled, hissed, and spat sparks. They felt warmer and closer than ever, as the light of the flames danced on their faces. Liddy brought their favorite refreshment, buttered bread to roast on the grate, along with warm cider to enjoy as Mother took up her needlepoint and as Father proceeded to give one of his lectures on safety and deportment.

"Never go to the river without an adult," he instructed us. "And never assume that frozen rivers or ponds are safe to walk on."

Whenever Father gave an admonition, he directed it to Peter as the eldest, or to his sister Sarah when it had special import for the girls. It was never necessary to address the younger children directly, for they immediately hushed and sat with eyes fixed on Father when he spoke. They all knew that he was laying down the rules of the family, and that there would be no questions.

The spring was always welcome, for it stayed light longer. In the late afternoon, when Father returned from visiting his patients, the family would often venture outdoors for a walk along the Thames. Whenever they approached Blackfriars jetty, they all had their assignments. The older children held their younger brothers' and sisters' hands while Father reminded them not to get too close to the water's edge. These were special family times. They jollied, they laughed, and they sang as they strode along the river. Then they would return to their home and enjoy the last of the sunlight, often with the windows open wide. If it was warm, they sat and talked around the hearth without lighting a fire. This, of course, made Liddy happy, for the hearth fires produced smoke and greasy soot, and Mother insisted on the room being cleaned every day. Mother did not allow soot to settle anywhere in her house for longer than 24 hours. For her, cleanliness was the highest of virtues. When Liddy called them to dinner, Mother, stationed at the washstand by the entrance to the dining room, made sure every family member was properly scrubbed. Following dinner, they returned to the salon for stories, games, and songs.

They also had parties with relatives and friends in this room, sometimes with music and dancing. On these occasions, the lane would be lined with horses, sedan chairs, and attendants and the house would be filled with finely dressed gentlemen and their ladies. Of course, the children too were decked out in their finest clothes. They would prance about and clap their hands as the musicians tuned up and couples lined up for a dance in this wonderful room.

So Peter mused, but though these reveries calmed him for a time, his mind kept racing back to the College interview. Those asses! Those blithering idiots! I am 20, a brilliant physician. Before I reached 18, I earned degrees in medicine from the Universities of Cambridge, Oxford, and Padua. Those arrogant and jealous fools had no right to talk to me that way. Surely, they know my Grandpapa and Uncle Peter invented the instrument that has saved the lives of so many mothers and infants in obstructed labors. They say I am not fit to be a member of the College of Physicians. They should recognize me for my accomplishments and my heritage; they should not be so callous.

"It's a travesty! An insult!" he shouted, and heard the words echo around the room as he sat slumped in his father's large chair.

And where was Father? It was torturous waiting for him to arrive. How can I tell him what happened? He knew his father would be as devastated as he. After all, his father and Uncle Peter had devoted much of their lives to preparing him for acceptance into the College of Physicians. It would be, in their minds, acceptance of them as well. Surely, his rejection would be an overwhelming disappointment for both of them. He dreaded the upcoming encounter with his father even more than the disastrous one he had just suffered with the College of Physicians.

He stared into the flames. He kept hearing their insulting words. In his whole life, he had never failed at anything, but today he was done in. The fire sputtered and crackled, sending forth spirals of steam. Another crackle spit a tiny coal skyward to land near his boot. He stomped it out. He repelled several more attacks from the spitting, hissing coals before another ember landed right next to his boot, but he was too overcome with fatigue to step on it, and watched it until it died. The battling flames were spell-binding, and they ultimately worked their magic. As he settled back in the big chair, his nostalgia finally subdued his ire and he began to doze. Then, as the angry fire continued to snarl and crackle loudly, he stirred, rubbed his eyes, and came back to the present.

His father was entering the salon. He sprang out of his chair to greet him. His father approached him directly and studied Peter closely as he faced him. Though he towered two to three inches above him, Peter did not feel like standing up very tall at this moment.

"How did the interview go, my son?" he demanded, instantly aware of his agitated and disheveled appearance.

"Father, I barely know how to begin. And the worst of it is that I have disappointed you and Uncle Peter. I have let you down miserably. It all happened so fast. This is the worst day of my life."

"Your face and your posture tell me something is very wrong. What is it, my son? Tell me your problem. It cannot be so grave. Was the interview so very difficult?"

"Horrible! They admitted that my education, examinations, and practice were beyond reproach, but they faulted me—no, they berated me—for what they called foppish attire! Those arrogant bastards told me I was not fit to be a member of the College."

"But, you will be a member?" insisted his Father with an air of suspicious doom. Usually it took several minutes for Peter the Younger to work into one of his frequent rages, but now his forehead was already furrowed, his jaw set, and his face ruby red. He leaned forward and sputtered, "You have to be more careful with those malevolent dunces at the College. Did you get them angry?"

"No, Father. Those arrogant and pompous fools dished it out and I had to take it. But, as you had advised me, I remained calm, mostly silent."

"They have wounded us once again. Your uncle and I have been disgraced."

"I am sorry for you and Uncle Peter, Father," he answered, "but I also have been humiliated. I have never failed at anything in my life. This is devastating for me."

"And what did they say about your membership?" his father demanded, almost shouting.

"They said that I must prove that I am worthy of being a proper and dignified member of the College. They will reconsider my application in two years," he responded.

"Two more years! That is ridiculous! Your uncle and I have worked so hard." His face was florid and his body was rigid. "This is the final straw. Yesterday someone again tried to steal the secret instrument, and today you are rejected by the Royal College!" He turned and stomped out of the room.

Stunned, Peter returned to his father's chair. He stared again at the fire, but now he had no intention of sleeping or dreaming, or wallowing in self-pity. Now he felt more like a Knight of the Round Table taking a solemn vow. His thoughts were clear:

My Father is bitterly disappointed, and I am sure Uncle Peter will be equally so. In truth, this appears to be a hopeless situation, but problems have never stopped me in the past. I am going to work so hard that those jealous old fools at the College will realize what a mistake they have made. They shall see Peter Chamberlen a member of the College of Physicians. And they shall be sorry for the humiliation they have heaped upon us.

* * *

Peter immediately started in practice with his father and Uncle Peter and soon was hard at work attending deliveries. With a combination of three degrees, his natural talent as a physician and his tireless work ethic, he quickly became a sought-after physician. He was already knowledgeable about the use of the secret instrument, as he had carried it around in a box for his father and Uncle Peter for many years. It was the key to the lying-in chamber. Peter knew it could also be the key to his fortune. In truth, there was wealth to be had in obstetric practice. His father and Uncle Peter charged patients according to their involvement in the delivery. A family that was wealthy and wanted a man-midwife present would be charged £10, because it might require staying in the home for a few days at the time of the expected labor. This was a very large sum, for his father and Uncle Peter paid their serving maids no more than £3 per annum. Usually, however, they charged less. Their most common request was to come to a home on a stand-by basis in case the midwife had trouble. They would then wait in a nearby room until the delivery was safely over. For this service they charged £2 or £3. Emergency calls were their forte. These generally entailed a lesser expenditure of time, however, and so they charged less, even though the situation might be direr. In such cases, they charged only £1 or, if the family was poor, nothing (Wilson 1995).

Chapter 22   Sarah Takes to Bed

Sarah had always been healthy. Even on those rare occasions when she became ill, she did so with a remarkable resilience. Once each winter, it seemed, she developed a runny nose, cough, and sore chest that lasted no more than one or two days and never interrupted her busy schedule. That is why it was so remarkable when on her 46th birthday in 1625 she took to her bed with illness.

Her condition was diagnosed as a malady of the kidneys. Though he was as busy as ever with his own patients, Peter the Younger visited Sarah many times a day, for this illness was very different and more severe than anything she had ever had. It had started suddenly a week earlier when she noted pain in her flanks and bloody urine. The next day she began to feel progressively weaker; then, as her strength diminished, she could only lie in her bed. From time to time, she shook with chills, followed by a sensation that she was burning up. The ache in her back was excruciating. Two physicians came to evaluate her, and even her learned father was called in as a consultant. Her brother, Gideon, had compounded special medications for her, but so far nothing had made her better. The pain raged on, and the condition appeared relentless. Her husband sat by her side, trying to cheer her up, but it was all he could do to stay composed himself. In spite of the best medical care possible, the disease finally claimed Sarah's life.

The loss of Sarah was devastating for the whole family. Peter the Younger was shaken the most, for their bond of love was stronger than iron. That Sarah should die first was something he had never considered. She had been his rock, his compass, and his precious friend through two decades. Feeling now only an enormous emptiness, and dwelling on his hatred of the College of Physicians, he became increasingly bitter. Nothing now seemed to go well for him.

For the children, the loss was as painful as anything they

had ever experienced. Sarah had always been such a dominant force in their lives, with her bright spirit, caring advice, and enveloping love. They all knew the void she had left could never be filled, but they slowly accepted that they had been blessed to be able to share her spirit for as long as they did. As time passed, the loss transformed into a beautiful memory of a lasting love shared so completely that surely it must be eternal. Whenever the family met, they talked fondly of the wonderful times they had shared with Sarah. But Peter the Younger would often seem lost in thought, overwhelmed by memories, and occasionally could be seen trying to hold back his tears.

Chapter 23   Bittersweet Victory - 1626

The loss of Sarah was replaced by her resilient spirit, still guiding her loved ones to work hard and to strive to do their best. Despite the problems the Chamberlens had experienced with the College of Physicians and the law, their practice prospered and Dr. Peter was very busy. Like his father and Uncle Peter before him, he enjoyed popularity with midwives because he was highly successful in converting obstructed labors into live-born births. But unlike his father and Uncle Peter, he had the advantage of three medical degrees, though he still lacked membership in the College. He was very popular at Court, for he was young, vital, and radiated an aura of supreme confidence. Under his uncle's careful guidance, he learned the protocol of Court life, and he never appeared at a function without appropriate, if not flamboyant, dress. His popularity with fellow physicians, however, was not quite as widespread, as he had had several run-ins with colleagues over patient management. He felt strongly that much of his unpopularity was the result of jealously. There was only one credential Peter was lacking, membership in the College of Physicians. The college officials had deliberately delayed that for five years. That is why he was so determined, or more likely possessed, when he returned to the Royal College of Physicians for another try at membership.

As Peter approached the College offices on July 26, 1626, he must have presented quite a sight, decked out in the latest fashion of the times. He was wearing bright colors and had a wide, white lace collar and frilly cuffs. He also sported silver buckles on his boots and an outrageous, extravagant, plumed hat. In spite of his controversial attire he was treated cordially and examined. Peter passed the exam, was approved for membership and elected. There was a small ceremony for new members. As Dr. Peter witnessed the conferring of memberships to two other physicians, none more than two years out of Oxford or Cambridge, and neither superior to him in talent, he must have realized what a great injustice the College had heaped upon him. He had received his medical degree from Padua 7 years earlier and was denied membership for almost a decade, all because of a foppish, plumed hat! How could those silly old fools have so brutally impeded his professional career? As he received his membership, he must have had very strong emotions about the extremely brutal way the College of Physicians had treated his father who now was so diminished he could not attend this event, and the cruelty heaped upon Uncle Peter by putting him in prison. Nonetheless, Peter pressed on and triumphed by carrying the name of Chamberlen to new heights in medicine.

Following his admittance to the College, a special honor was bestowed on him. Dr. Peter was asked to perform the annual anatomy dissections for the Barber-Surgeons Company, a task in which he was highly skilled because of his experience at the University of Padua. There was no lack of dissection material, for there were always many unclaimed bodies in London.

Panoramic view of London looking north between Southwark
Bridge and London Bridge, Gideon Yates c.1831

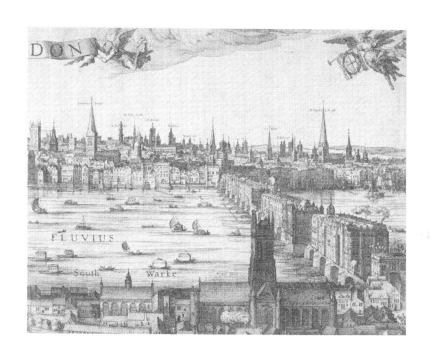

Panoramic view of London looking north between Southwark
Bridge and London Bridge, Gideon Yates c.1831

Chapter 24   Peter the Younger's Death

Peter the Elder continued to introduce his nephew to the high-born at Court. Dr. Peter enjoyed mingling with these interesting people, for they always seemed to be talking about important issues. Their dress was splendid, so, not to appear out of place, he kept visiting his tailor to assure that he was frocked in the latest finery. A plumed hat, silver buckles for his boots, and even a silver-trimmed walking stick were adornments that he liked. As he moved with increasing ease in this high company, he knew that the College would not approve of his attire, but he also knew that his manner of dress at Court was not the real reason they had rejected him for membership in the College. They had denied him, he was certain, because he was a Chamberlen.

Over time, their family was able to take the tragic loss of Sarah in their stride, largely because they had so many wonderful memories of her. For Dr. Peter, the mere mention of her name evoked feelings of serenity and contentment. This was in marked contrast to any memory of dealings with the College of Physicians. Yet Peter's bitter disappointment over their rejection of him was never as profound as his father's. It had become increasingly clear that Peter the Younger's *raison d'être* was to see his son become a member of the College, a thing he himself could never achieve. Because this had not happened, he became more and more disconsolate. Obsessed by his son's failure, Peter the Younger at first tried to stay busy, attending many deliveries in order to stay active, but he was still increasingly distressed. His unhappiness was made greater by Sarah's untimely death, as he was utterly unprepared for losing her. She had given him the strength to face the problems of the world, and he missed her enormously. Frequently, he started to speak to her, only to turn and realize that no one was there.

Peter the Younger was now 54 years old, and he realized that he would never see his dream for his son come true. He fretted constantly over this situation, losing weight and becoming irritable and withdrawn. As he sank deeper into melancholy, he started to blame Peter III, in part, for his woes. At this time he stopped attending patients and would not let anyone even mention the College of Physicians in his home. His children repeatedly tried in vain to comfort him as he became increasingly irascible. Finally, his bitterness became so great that he could not stand to remain in London, the seat of his disappointment, and so he retired to Downe in Kent. There he spent much of his day in bed, listless and unkempt, taking no care for his appearance or his health. In early 1626, at age 54, his life started to ebb away, as he mumbled obscenities about the College and appeared no longer to recognize his surroundings. It was in this diminished state that he died in his sleep. He was buried on August 16, 1626 three weeks after Peter became a member of the College.

Chapter 25   Passing the Torch

In 1625, King James died and his son Charles, Scone of Scotland, was crowned King, bringing great hope of easing the longstanding strife between England and Scotland. A year earlier, Charles had married, by proxy, Henrietta Maria, a 14-year-old French princess with hooded eyes, a long nose, and protruding teeth. Now she had invaded London with her retinue: a gaggle of courtiers, a bishop, 29 priests, an aristocratic nanny, and more than 400 attendants, all sharing Somerset House (Aslet 1999, page 94). Raised in the French court, the new Queen proved to be spirited and charming, but she was also a devout Catholic, and that was always a worry for English Protestants who remembered the treacherous days of Bloody Queen Mary.

Because Peter the Elder was so respected as a royal physician, he was able to introduce his nephew to the new royal circles. As attendees at Court, Peter the Elder and his nephew would have heard tidbits of news concerning the vicissitudes of the royal couple's marital state. Their fluency in French was of course very useful as they strove to keep up on the intrigues.

Meanwhile at Court, King Charles and Queen Henrietta Maria, with little in common, were unhappy during their early years of marriage. King Charles finally ejected Henrietta Maria's entire retinue, which by this time had grown to nearly 600. Initially furious, the Queen came to appreciate the wisdom of her husband's decision, as she learned how freely some of her attendants had plundered her wealth.

Under the mantle of royalty, Henrietta Maria metamorphosed into to a lovely regal Queen. Her relationship with the King improved, and in 1628, at age 18, she became pregnant. Since she and the King both loved children, they were elated and looked forward to the birth of their first child.

According to *The Court and Times of Charles I* "The Queen mis-carried of her first child. She had neither mid-wife nor physician about her, only the poor town mid-wife of Greenwich was sent for who swooned with fear as soon as she was brought into the Queen's chamber so as she was forced presently to be carried out; and Chamberlayne the surgeon was he alone that did the part of a midwife. This took place in 1628 (Birch 1848)."

In keeping with the royal tradition, the Queen had retired to Greenwich in the sixth month of her pregnancy. The Queen's House was situated a short walk from the Thames. Behind the royal residence were magnificent gardens and a grassy park-like setting rising up a steep hill. Following a walk in her hilly gardens, the Queen began to have contractions and bleeding. Mrs. Dexter, the local Greenwich midwife, must have passed the Queen's House innumerable times for it is one of the most prominent architectural structures and dominated the landscape in Greenwich. But passing and entering are two entirely different activities. For Mrs. Dexter it would have been highly unlikely that she would have ever entered the Queen's House except for a twist of fate. When the Queen began to experience pain and vaginal bleeding, Mrs. Dexter was summoned at once to attend the Queen and was rushed to the residence by a royal messenger. As she entered, she must have been awestruck by the sumptuousness of the murals, tapestries, and paintings adorning the walls. Never before in the presence of royalty, she was terrified. Mrs. Dexter was led promptly to the Queen's bedchamber. Upon entering the room, the poor midwife, overcome with awe and terror, swooned and had to be carried out bodily. By this time, Peter the Elder had arrived from London, expecting only to oversee the delivery, but now he was greeted by a frightened and anxious staff. All of the attendants were speaking French. They rushed him to a hallway, where King Charles greeted him cordially, but hurriedly. He instructed Peter the Elder that "at all costs, the Queen's life had to be saved (Aslet 1999)."

Then Peter the Elder was taken directly to the Queen's bedchamber, where he found her in severe distress and pain. He addressed her in French, which comforted her, and tried to reassure her while he assessed her condition. He spoke calmly and soothingly, but he knew the situation was worrisome for the birth of an extremely premature infant was at hand.

As Peter the Elder prepared for the delivery, the Queen had an irresistible impulse to bear down and passed a lifeless baby boy. He was immediately handed to an attendant priest and christened Charles–James. Peter the Elder attempted to comfort the Queen by telling her how bravely she had performed. As he spoke to her, still in her native tongue, and amid her devastating loss, Queen Henrietta Maria found herself so pleased with her capable French-speaking man-midwife that she assured him she should want no births in the future without his assistance.

Charles–James was carried by boat up the Thames to Westminster Abbey and buried that night. Superstitious Henrietta Maria never returned to Greenwich to have a baby, and she was to have many (Aslet 1999, page 94).

Two years later, Peter the Elder, now appointed as Physician-in-Ordinary to Court, was summoned to Somerset House in London because Queen Henrietta Maria was in labor. On this occasion, he invited his nephew, Dr. Peter, to accompany him. Peter the Elder explained that the superstitious Queen had refused to return to Greenwich for childbirth after the tragedy of losing her first-born, Charles–James. In any event, London was more favorable for them for Greenwich was a considerable distance and often a rough trip downstream on the Thames.

When they arrived at Somerset House for the delivery, they were immediately admitted and led by an excited, French-speaking entourage to the salon, where King Charles was waiting impatiently. They bowed to the King and noted at least twenty other persons sitting around the perimeter of the room. They both offered a polite nod to the assembled crowd. As the King spoke directly to Peter the Elder, the onlookers seemed to lean forward in unison to hear what His Highness had to say. Dr. Peter recognized several of the people from Court. The others he assumed were the officials needed to attest to the authenticity of the birth. The King was cordial and nervous but direct. He said that the Queen was having strong pains, and he was concerned lest the outcome might be a repeat of the Greenwich tragedy. Peter the Elder wisely temporized by saying he anticipated a favorable outcome. He explained that her prior labor two years earlier had occurred after the Queen had been walking in her hilly gardens; in this pregnancy, at his direction, she had avoided such strenuous activity and was now at term.

As they entered the Queen's bedchamber, the gossips immediately locked the doors. Peter the Elder and Dr. Peter bowed to the Queen and returned her greeting in French, which brought a smile to her face. Her next contraction made it apparent that her labor was active, for the pains lasted more than a minute. The gossips scurried around the room trying to comfort the Queen, while Peter the Elder assured her that the outcome would be favorable and that he had brought his physician nephew to help. In actuality, it was 29 year-old Dr. Peter who performed the delivery, with his uncle standing at his side (Aveling 1882). You can imagine how overawed he felt to deliver a baby who someday might be King of England. It was Queen Henrietta Maria's first live baby and, fortunately for Dr. Peter, the labor and delivery were relatively normal. The secret instrument stayed in its box. The baby was to be named Charles. As soon as he was delivered, he was swaddled and handed to the Queen, who kissed him and cuddled him for a very short while, for he had to be presented to the King and the myriad of witnesses who would attest to the birth of an

133

heir to the throne.

On the occasion of the delivery, Dr. Peter was honored to be introduced to the official royal family physician, Theodore Turquet de Mayerne, a man nearing his 60th year. A brilliant clinician, he was convinced that his methods, though somewhat "modern," had the sanctions of Galen and Hippocrates. Dr. Turquet de Mayerne applied chemical principles to humoral medicine (a branch that posited that an excess or deficiency of the four distinct bodily fluids influences one's temperament and health), and added a greater empiricism to the more rational approach. He was highly regarded in England and abroad, so Peter was most fortunate that he was cordial and seemed to approve of him immediately. Perhaps, that was not surprising, since Turquet de Mayerne was related to his father-in-law, Dr. de Laune. Whatever the reason for his good will, this was an auspicious day for Dr. Peter for the torch had been passed.

Chapter 26   Fellowship in the College

Becoming a member of the Royal College of Physicians for Dr. Peter had been a burning desire. But now a more exalted position lay ahead, that of Fellowship of the College, signifying accomplishments and professional stature. It was totally predictable that he would not rest until he had attained that honor. A fellowship position became vacant some 17 months after he become a member of the College. Dr. Peter competed against Dr. Oxenbridge for the position. Although they both wanted the position and both had achievements to deserve that honor, on November 22, 1627 the fellowship was conferred on Dr. Oxenbridge as he was a much older man. On the 29th of March 1628, Dr. Peter's fortunes changed as another fellowship became available and he was elected by a majority of the votes but there was one serious proviso. The President was directed to gravely admonish Dr. Peter for his frivolous mode of dress and not to admit him until he conformed.

* * *

"I have requested this personal interview, because we have reviewed your application, and frankly we have some concerns. Your education is excellent and we congratulate you on that. In addition, we must admit that you have had some degree of success in your practice. But I must emphasize to you that fellowship in the Royal College of Physicians signifies more than mere success in the world. This institution was established by charter of King Henry VIII himself more than a century ago. We are professional men. We have the highest standards of dress and deportment in addition to the highest standards of practice. We recognize that through the efforts of your Uncle you have spent a great deal of time at Court. While that is not a matter for us to judge, your manner of dress seems foppish, and not at all in keeping with that of a distinguished man of the medical profession. If we were to approve your fellowship, we would be sanctioning a serious breach in deportment."

Peter indicated, as the President had stated, that he had the most excellent education and training. He protested. "It is not surprising that I am welcome at Court, for I had developed talents that even the nobility recognized as valuable in difficult deliveries. Therefore, I dressed so that I was appropriately attired when I visited royalty. Anything less would be disrespectful."

"That may be true, but your role as a fellow of the Royal College is as a professional man, not a courtesan. We are conservative in dress and deportment. You should be wearing full morning dress, not some foppish costume. You look like a peacock, not a physician! You should follow the example of some of your more distinguished and experienced colleagues. You disregard all propriety."

Peter took a deep breath and tried to remain composed. He drew on all of the wisdom and experience of his mentors, for to date their counsel had always translated into success. He assumed a very uncharacteristic stance, and remained silent.

After a pause, the President observed that he was not going to comment and said. "So, in conclusion, we want you to mend your ways. Prove to us that you are worthy of being a dignified representative of our profession."

* * *

The College must have considered the President's admonition very effective and Dr. Peter's compliance very outstanding as some days later April 7th Day of Our Lord 1628 after taking the oath to the King and the College he was admitted fellow of the College, fulfilling his deceased father's dreams, the obsession that had completely overtaken his life and appears to have caused his death.

Certainly, fellowship in the College of Physicians conferred enormous professional and social status to Dr. Peter. He was a 27 year old physician with three medical diplomas, a regular member the courts of King James, and now King Charles I, and recently a new fellow of the prestigious College of Physicians.

Chapter 27   Jane Myddelton

In 1628, Dr. Peter was a frequent attendee at Court. As such, he had many invitations to attend elegant parties in London. Imagine how this pleased him because he was able to dress fashionably, mingle with London society, and associate with interesting people who talked of more than the humdrum happenings of daily life. He also had the opportunity to meet many eligible young ladies. During one of these gatherings, he was presented to Jane Myddelton. Miss Myddelton was strikingly attractive, possessed all the social graces, and seemed to enjoy talking with people. She was tall, with a pleasing figure and an inviting smile.

Jane was the daughter of Hugh Myddelton, a man of Welsh descent who had become quite wealthy as an engineer and goldsmith in London. Among his accomplishments were serving as an Alderman and Member of Parliament for his town of Denbigh in north Wales and participating in many successful financial ventures. He was best known for completing an extraordinary feat, the New River Project, which had brought potable water directly into London homes for the first time. For those fortunate enough to be subscribers to this project, it meant they no longer had to drink the impure water of the Thames. These were modern times; the subscribers had the luxury of fresh, potable water, delivered through a quill directly to their homes.

For centuries, people had been dumping garbage, human waste, and animal entrails into the Thames and its tributaries. This same water was delivered to many homes by barrel casks and others by lead pipes. Frankly, the water was foul.

By 1600, the population of London had swelled to 200,000, all needing a source of better water. In that year, Edmund Colthurst proposed a plan to the Corporation of London to bring water from the Lee River in Hertfordshire to a giant reservoir in Stoke Newington, and thence by a canal to London. The plan was accepted in 1602, but the New River Project was then put on hold while landowners considered the effect it might have on irrigation and Lee River navigation. Unfortunately, Queen Elizabeth, the project's leading supporter, died before Colthurst could be given a license to begin work.

But as luck would have it, King James then became interested in the project, expressing concern for "the poor people of London who were forced to use foul and unwholesome water." In 1604, the King granted Colthurst permission to proceed, provided that he finish within seven years and that the canal be no more than six feet wide. The King even put some of his own money into the project. The next year Colthurst completed 3 miles of the canal at a cost of £200. He applied to the Corporation for more funding, but to no avail, so the project came to a halt, languishing for several years.

In 1609, the Corporation awarded Myddelton the contract; perhaps because he was an engineer by training, a Member of Parliament, independently wealthy, had participated in numerous merchant undertakings, and had been the Royal Jeweler to King James. London was only 20 miles away from the reservoir, as the crow flies, but they had to follow the contour of the land, assuring a constant flow of water without pumps, using only gravity. This necessitated creation of a 38-mile river. They completed the project in 5 years. There was a great ceremony marking the opening, attended by King James himself and Thomas Myddelton, the Lord Mayor, who was Hugh's brother. The river provided a source of clean water to Londoners, and a source of considerable ongoing wealth for the Myddelton family.

Hugh Myddelton was involved in many projects and also was indirectly involved in an undertaking that was linked to the slave trade. Nonetheless, he was a very honest and influential man.

Peter wasted no time in wooing and winning the lovely Jane Myddelton. Dressed in his finest daytime attire, he called at the Myddelton home in Bush Hill, hoping to visit with Jane in person. Peter Chamberlen met Hugh Myddelton and developed a friendship with him, but he also visited with Jane and quickly was convinced that she was the love of his life.

In 1629, Peter married Jane Myddelton. The wedding was a major social event for London. Each had so many family members and friends, including many of the nobility, that they had an enormous wedding party at the Myddelton home. Covered coaches with handsome horse teams lined the street. The fanciest dresses and male attire abounded as the party convened. The wines were specially selected by Hugh Myddelton himself and the banquet was sumptuous, with endless courses, capped by heaping platters of capon and venison. Two orchestras played, and the dancing continued late into the evening.

The newlyweds lived in Blackfriars in a home that was a wedding gift from Jane's father. Hugh also gave Jane a wedding gift of a share in the New River. Peter had always lived an enjoyable life but his circumstances improved considerably with Jane for they were very much in love and she provided many attributes to help him in his busy career.

One year later, Jane was expecting their first child, and they were reflecting on names. If it were a girl, they would probably have named her Jane, or perhaps Sarah, after Peter's sainted mother. If it were a boy, the challenge would be greater, for Peter owed so much of his success to his father and Uncle that the name Peter would have to be considered. The fact that there were already three Peter Chamberlens, however, complicated the situation, and they chose not to perpetuate this tradition by creating a fourth. Ultimately, the choice was not difficult for Hugh Myddelton had been a major influence in their lives, as well as a great friend. They dined with him often, he remained very close to his daughter Jane, and he had made them even wealthier than they might have been without him, even with Peter's lucrative practice. And so, as their first-born was a boy, not surprisingly, they named him Hugh.

Chapter 28   Peter the Elder's and Hugh Myddelton's Deaths

Peter the Elder, now over seventy years old, appeared to be aging with grace. His hair had gone gray and he was slightly stooped, yet his wit prevailed. Nevertheless, he seemed to be losing some of his vigor and commonly complained of fatigue. He found that his responsibilities were becoming too much for him. He had been planning for the past year how he would further Peter's career, and so he took advantage of one of his visits to Court to propose Dr. Peter to Queen Henrietta Maria as his replacement. Dr. Turquet de Mayerne added his approval of Dr. Peter as a royal physician. With these two respected physicians supporting him, how could he lose?

With another Peter Chamberlen securely positioned to perform royal deliveries, Peter the Elder retired to his brother's small estate at Downe in Kent. He did not live far away, but the trip took over four hours. His wife, Anne, had died earlier, so now he lived with his only daughter, Dr. Peter's cousin Esther, and her daughter, Anne Cargill. Peter the Elder's life in retirement was rather sedate. He read books, gardened, entertained family and old friends, and spent many evenings telling stories to young Anne, his grandchild. Peter missed seeing him daily, as they were the best of friends as well as colleagues.

When Dr. Peter learned that his uncle had suddenly died, he was overcome with grief and hurried immediately to Downe. Since Peter the Elder was a very important person in the kingdom, the family would be expected to arrange for an appropriate funeral, and this responsibility fell mainly on Peter. They sent black crêpe to family members and close friends to drape their homes and doors and had tickets printed for admission to the funeral. Many Huguenots came from London and Southampton to pay their respects. They were joined by Royals and nobles, as well as many of Peter the Elder's ordinary patients, swelling the attendance to over 500.

As they left Downe, Dr. Peter probably had the sobering realization that he was now the only person in the world with knowledge of the secret instrument. History would prove that he was a very dedicated guardian.

After Peter the Elder's death, the months passed quickly as Peter immersed himself again in his practice. Then one morning a messenger arrived telling the Chamberlens to go immediately to the home of Hugh Myddelton.

They arrived just as he was dying. Hugh had a powerful frame and had always looked hale and hearty, but now as he lay on his bed he was pale and barely responsive. Jane sat at her father's side and held his hand. She said soothing things to her beloved father, but she realized that she was losing him. The physicians came and went, but Jane sat stroking his hands. At last Hugh lost his battle and quietly passed away. Jane and Peter had suffered another profound loss.

The calling ceremony was on the first day and the funeral the next. The funeral was long and formal with many testimonials from friends and government officials. More than 600 people attended, out of friendship and respect. Jane greeted and talked to everyone who came to call, while her heart must been shattered by the death of this great man.

In his will, Hugh left £500 and a share of the New River enterprise to Jane's younger sisters and brothers. Hugh indicated that Jane had received her inheritance at the time of her marriage. £10 was given each to Jane and Peter in order to purchase rings. Jane, already quite wealthy, was delighted to see her siblings do well. The loss of her father was poignant, but somehow Jane could see a bright side; she still had the second best man in the world as her husband.

Chapter 29　　　Court Appointment

1632 was a wonderful year for Dr. Peter and Uncle Gideon. The Worshipful Society of Apothecaries of London opened its offices at Cobham House in the old Blackfriars' guest house with Gideon de Laune presiding. Peter attended, for Uncle Gideon was one of his favorite friends and, of course, he reminded him strongly of his mother, Sarah.

Dr. Peter was officially appointed as the Physician-in-Ordinary to the Court and he immediately sent letters of thanks and appreciation to Dr. Theodore Turquet de Mayerne and his father's father-in-law, Dr. William de Laune. In all of his life, Peter had never felt he could be held back. Now his hard work and devotion had earned him respect and admiration. When he walked the streets of London, he was well-known; gentlemen doffed their hats to him and he enjoyed the admiration. He was sought out for advice in all manner of things and his professional life soared. Life could not have been better.

Peter's efforts to incorporate the midwives of London now consumed much of his time since he no longer had the help of his Uncle. He had formalized the academic curriculum for the midwives and was now ready to expand the program. Dr. Theodore Mayerne de Turquet and Sir Martin Lister, believing the incorporation could save many lives, had agreed to serve on the faculty. Prospects for incorporation were looking favorable. What could prevent him from success?

Chapter 30   Petition of King Charles

Dr. Peter continued to expand the organization of midwives, the purpose being to raise their level of practice. Peter the Elder was greatly missed during the teaching sessions for they had worked as a team. Now Peter doubled his efforts to incorporate the midwives and was recruiting the best in London. The monthly education meetings, followed by an elegant meal and bright conversation, were well recognized throughout the profession. Each month more and more midwives presented themselves as hopeful candidates for their group.

Although Peter the Elder had been the partner and participated in both attempts to educate and incorporate the midwives (1616 and 1634), it appears that Dr. Peter and his father, Peter the Younger, were the driving forces. In both attempts, the training and entertaining of the midwives took place in their homes. Peter the Elder had died by the time of the actual petition in 1634. In all of the documents of the College of Physicians and the Bishops it was Peter the Younger and, subsequently, Dr. Peter who were referenced.

It became Dr. Peter's obsession to incorporate all midwifery in London with himself as director. If he could accomplish this goal, the Archbishop who had neglected the teaching and oversight of midwives would then have little or no authority. The standards of midwifery in London, and all of England for that matter, would improve and countless lives might be saved.

After Peter the Elder and Dr. Peter delivered the first live baby for King Charles and Queen Henrietta Maria, Dr. Peter became a privileged friend and confidante of the King. This proved a most helpful association, for in 1633 he was able to convince Charles that incorporation of midwives would be good for London, as it would provide the educational and practice standards then sorely lacking under the authority of the Anglican Church. Besides, he argued, he had the secret instrument to help midwives when in trouble. Dr. Peter had gained the support of King Charles. His endorsement meant that the incorporation would happen; it was only a question of when.

Chapter 31   The Midwives Organize

Recently, however, Peter's prospects had dimmed somewhat; those midwives who were not in the Chamberlen cadre had become well organized and were aggressively opposing the Chamberlens' plan. Hester Shaw, an independent midwife, became a fierce attacker of the Chamberlens. Seeking allies in this struggle, she tried to enlist Mrs. Whipp, a stalwart though middling midwife. Wealthy and socially prominent, Mrs. Whipp was searching for a *raison d'être*. At first, she was uninterested in joining forces with Hester, for she considered her sharp-tongued and commonplace. Over time, however, Hester succeeded in convincing Mrs. Whipp that they would make a good team. They agreed that the Episcopal system of licensing midwives was flawed. They also knew that the Archbishop's criteria for licensing were erratic and that midwife supervision was poor at best, but they were convinced that the intrusion of the Chamberlens into their all-women trade was a greater evil.

Under the leadership of Mrs. Hester Shaw and Mrs. Whipp, they met frequently and conspired to overturn the Chamberlens' attempts at incorporation. Although the surroundings and food were no match for the Chamberlens' fare, the fervor was. They collected donations from the members to hire a solicitor, and he was on the attack. They must have realized that the Chamberlens had already convinced the King. The solicitor advised them that the only way to stop the Chamberlens' petition to incorporate the midwives of London was to have their own petition. The London midwives relished the idea that they might take charge of their own destiny. They were angry at the threat of male midwives taking their livelihood and invading the all-woman process of childbirth. The very threat enkindled more fervor, determination, and donations.

Together, Mrs. Shaw and Mrs. Whipp continued the

monthly meetings while scheming the downfall of the Chamberlens. Before long, they had organized more than 60 London midwives to oppose "the Chamberlen attempt to take over their livelihood and their practice." With the help of their solicitor, Mrs. Shaw and Mrs. Whipp made a formal petition to block the Chamberlen attempt to incorporate. Knowing that the Chamberlens had a troubled history with the College of Physicians, the petition was directed, not to the Archbishop, but to the College, the overseers of the Chamberlens' professional credentials. Mrs. Shaw and Whipp seemed determined beyond reason to thwart the incorporation (Aveling 1882).

Chapter 32   Incorporation of Midwives – 1634

The College informed Dr. Peter Chamberlen of the midwives petition and instructed him to attend a special meeting to decide the issue. Though he was concerned, he had no reason to doubt the outcome. With all that his late Uncle Peter and he had done to educate and train midwives, together with the support of King Charles, he had no reason to imagine the Royal College of Physicians would give any credibility to Mrs. Shaw and Mrs. Whipp. After all, he was now a fellow of the College in good standing; moreover, it could not be denied that midwifery in London was in a sorry state overall. The meeting at the College took place on August 28, 1634. The following is the Registrar's record of what took place:

> Mrs. Hester Shawe and Mrs. Whipp presented a petition to the College; it being read, it appeared merely to concern Dr. Chamberlayne, concerning the making of Midwifes a Corporation to the College and himself to be governour of it. Dr. Chamberlayne desired to have the Copy of the petition but it was denied him till he should deliver into the College his propositions made to the King; or that he should submit his cause to the Censors, which he refused. (Aveling 1882, page 34)

As the proceedings began, Mrs. Shaw and Mrs. Whipp were invited to express their concerns. They at once charged that Dr. Chamberlen was not to be trusted with any project for midwife regulation because he had a conflict of interest: as a man-midwife he had a financial motive in being called to cases in which female midwives could not manage, and thus more to gain from keeping them ignorant and incompetent than from encouraging them to improve their practice (Donnison 1977). For this same reason, they claimed, my "dear daughters," which is to say, the midwives he had organized and trained, "...oftentimes by their bungling and untoward usage of their women, and oftentimes through ignorance do send for him, when it is none of his worke, and so to the damage of the partie both in body and purse do highly increase his profit."

They charged further that the midwives who supported his proposal were being bribed with entertainment such as "venison, wine, and other delicates." At the same time, they said, he "would not repair unto such women as are distressed whose midwives had refused to conform themselves to him (Graham 1960, page 184)." Finally, they argued that because he lacked experience in normal labors, it was arrogant and presumptuous of him to propose to instruct midwives. They claimed he had performed no deliveries "without the use of instruments by extraordinary violence in desperate occasions (Donnison 1977). In short, they disparaged his motives, integrity, and competence.

Shaw and Whipp also took the opportunity to complain that Dr. Chamberlen had made the midwives meet at his house once a month, which they said he had no authority to do, and that he was bent on having the sole licensing power "out of an opinion of himself and his own ability in the Art of Midwifery."

After such a scurrilous attack, he was furious and almost speechless. He regained his composure enough to state his conviction that incorporation of the midwives would improve teaching and raise the standards of midwifery practice in London, but his words were apparently falling on deaf ears. In short, the College of Physicians ruled in favor of Mrs. Shaw and Mrs. Whipp, and indicated that they would not support his proposal.

Still reeling from his defeat at the College of Physicians, Dr. Peter was summoned to appear, on October 22, 1634 to a full dress inquiry of the incorporation of midwives at the Palace of Lambeth, with the all-powerful Archbishop of Canterbury, William Laud, and the Bishop of London presiding. These were the ecclesiastical authorities who then controlled the licensing of midwives. While Peter recognized their authority, he had every reason to believe they would in turn recognize his substantial contributions to childbirth care. It could not be denied that he had superior knowledge of the subject as well as extensive clinical experience and a reputation for excellence acknowledged throughout England and Europe. Furthermore, he had spent more than a decade helping and educating midwives to improve childbirth care in London. Below is the scene as I imagine it.

* * *

"Dr. Chamberlen, Mrs. Shaw and Mrs. Whipp, duly licensed and practicing midwives in London, have made strong arguments against your proposal to monopolize the licensing and training of midwives in this City. Indeed, they have testified against your behavior and intentions with conviction.

"Dr. Chamberlen, you have no authority over the midwives of London and its jurisdiction. You may have educated many midwives, and to that end you may even have done the women and children of London a fair service. Nevertheless, I see no reason for granting you or your relatives any authority over the midwives of this City. There is no precedent for it in any commonwealth. There is no compelling reason for an exception here."

Dr. Chamberlen had one last attempt: "If you would allow me to have Dr. Theodore Turquet de Mayerne and Sir Martin Lister testify on behalf of the incorporation and education, I am sure you would change your mind." Unfortunately, it fell on deaf ears. The outcome was overwhelmingly in favor of Mrs. Shaw and Mrs. Whipp. They had succeeded in defeating his attempt to gain control of the midwives. Furthermore, His Excellency had humiliated Dr. Chamberlen by demanding that he obtain a midwifery license, himself.

* * *

It had been the worst day of Peter's life, worse even than the day he had been rejected for membership by the College. He did not take defeat lightly, and unfortunately he let it smolder in the recesses of his mind. He was too proud to talk about it with friends or colleagues and the onus of the defeat continued to grow.

Chapter 33   Reaction to Defeat

Dr. Peter was a resilient man. When faced with adversity, he showed tenacity and industry by burying himself in work and projects. His practice continued to do well as his fame spread and indeed, word of his skills and prowess had passed far beyond the continent. In 1636 he was visited by an emissary of the Czar of Russia, and, in short order, he was offered a position as the physician to the Czar. The Czar himself sent King Charles a handwritten letter asking that he permit Dr. Peter to accept this offer if Dr. Chamberlen wished (Aveling 1882, page 33).

The Chamberlens talked of this prospect many times before they made their decision. Jane was by nature more adventurous than Peter, more willing to dare something entirely new. Although life in London was splendid for them, she was apparently willing to give it all over to try the life of the Russian Court. Peter was not as eager, for his professional life in London was very successful and he could not imagine having as much satisfaction serving as personal physician to the Czar. But in the end they agreed it was an opportunity they could not ignore.

Great preparations were made for their departure for Archangel, the Russian port on the far Northern Sea, which was the way from London to Moscow. At the last moment, however, King Charles, unwilling to relinquish Peter's services, wrote back to excuse himself for refusing the Czar's request, upon the grounds that a native Russian, Dr. Elmston, had returned to his own country, and so was capable of filling the office of physician to the Czar (Aveling 1882, page 32).

As they readjusted to prospects of life in England, they decided to expand their sphere with a country home. In 1637, Dr. Peter heard of a manor house in Maldon that belonged to Sir Crammer Harris and was for sale. He was able to secure a good price and they became owners of a sizeable country estate.

Maldon, an ancient Royal Charter town situated on the Blackwater River on the east coast of Essex, is some 45 miles from London. A Saxon settlement famous for a battle fought there in 991, when Vikings crossed the North Sea, sailed up the Blackwater River, and invaded the town, Maldon survived and flourished.

In 1637, the port of Maldon was busy and prosperous, a prime destination of the sailing barges that plied the waters of the North Sea and the English Channel between Holland and England. With its safe harbor, it was the transit point for farm goods from the rich East Anglian soil, which provided plentiful crops of wheat, rapeseed, beans, and potatoes.

Away from the busy port area, they found Maldon a quiet town with gently rolling hills and winding lanes with hedgerows. Maldon's High Street ran from Hythe Quay up to Market Street, which wended its way down a steep hill to the river. Numerous large manor houses and beautiful churches, such as All Saints and Saint Peter's, graced the landscape. Moot Hall was the seat of the local government. The Jolly Sailor, a pub on the Hythe Quay, was a favorite spot for an occasional evening's entertainment. The town at that time boasted three hotels: The Swan and The King's Head on High Street and The Blue Boar, the oldest, dating back to the 14th century.

Their new home was three miles from the center of Maldon in a village called Woodham Mortimer. Their house, Woodham Mortimer Hall, was situated on the London Road overlooking Maldon and the Blackwater River. They had 24 rooms and several outbuildings, and they were somewhat of a landmark.

Nestled next to their home stood Saint Margaret's Church, which was frequented by many of the local noblemen who were members of the Church of England. As nonconformists, the Chamberlens attended a church in Maldon. They grew to love this area, a welcome contrast to

Woodham Mortimer Hall (Aveling 1882)

the bustle of London, but of course Peter's professional life still took him to London often. Since it took a full day to travel between London and Maldon on the poorly kept roads, even using their fine new coach with a team of horses, it was best to plan visits to be a week at a time. Dr. Chamberlen's currency was down but one would never count him out.

Chapter 34   Dr. Peter's Family

Jane managed their home and the children with great skill and aplomb. It was well that she did, because they were eventually to have 11 sons and two daughters. First came Hugh in 1630. From his infancy, they knew Hugh to be a special child, for he was inquisitive, alert, and very social. Jane was thrilled with her firstborn, and that proved fortunate because the children were to arrive in a steady procession thereafter.

Next were Paul in 1632 and John in 1635, with Elizabeth, Thomas, Richard, Peter, Philip, and Abraham following in rapid succession. All were healthy, active, and diligent in their studies. The outstanding one was Hugh, for he learned with alacrity and in turn helped to teach his younger brothers and sisters. In striving to provide the best care for their children, they were blessed with skillful servants, who were brought from the Myddelton home and thus were very well trained. They had nursemaids and tutors, and life with this large family was effortless, or so it seemed because Jane was so clever at organizing the household.

Jane and Peter cherished their quiet time together. In the evenings after the children were abed, they would sit before a fire in the salon and read stories and poems to each other. Jane's favorites were the "Holy Sonnets" of John Donne and Edmund Spenser's *Fairie Queene*. Dr. Peter's were the tales of King Arthur and his Round Table, as related by Sir Thomas Malory, but Peter liked Shakespeare's sonnets best. He often read aloud his Sonnet 29, "When in disgrace with fortune and men's eyes," since it had particular meaning for him. He also loved his Sonnet 18, "Shall I compare thee to a summer's day?" which expressed so perfectly his feeling's for Jane. But when he felt capricious, he would intone Sonnet 130 to her:

> My mistress' eyes are nothing like the sun;
> Coral is far more red than her lips' red,

If snow be white, why then her breasts are dun;
If hairs be wires, black wires grow on her head.
I have seen roses damasked, red and white,
But no such roses see I in her cheeks;
And in some perfumes is there more delight
Than in the breath that from my mistress reeks.
I love to hear her speak, yet well I know
That music hath a far more pleasing sound,
I grant I never saw a goddess go;
My mistress when she walks, treads on the ground.
And yet, by heaven, I think my love as rare
As any she belied with false compare.

Chapter 35   The War Years

England enjoyed many years of peace and prosperity under good Queen Elizabeth and King James I, but things were about to change. King Charles I believed that the king was divinely appointed to rule. He hated going to Parliament to haggle over taxes and therefore did not assemble Parliament for over a decade, depending rather on his royal wealth and holdings to finance his wars and Court. A mounting tension between the King and Parliament threatened peace.

The King was intelligent, serious, and well-intentioned but often unwise. His vivacious and elegant Queen Henrietta Maria might have preferred a livelier Court, but the King established one that was stately and proper. Though raised a Presbyterian and not himself a man of extravagant taste, the King came to despise the dour and joyless Puritans who were striving to strip the English Church of any remaining color and ceremony. Perhaps in this he was influenced by his wife, who had never abandoned her Catholic faith. Parliament was composed increasingly of Puritans, and the King's lavish lifestyle was an affront to them; it was not surprising that a wide rift developed between Parliament and the King. The only thing they could agree upon at Hampton Court was a new translation of the Bible.

In 1633 William Laud, Bishop of Canterbury, and King Charles had tried to impose the Anglican Book of Common Prayer on the Presbyterian Scots, who objected mightily and after a time rebelled. Charles finally had to go north to raise an army to put down the Scots. Since he desperately needed money to pay his troops, in 1640, after an 11-year hiatus, he was forced to reconvene Parliament to vote funds. The result was a bitter confrontation.

Oliver Cromwell, a country gentleman from Huntingdon, until then had been an inconspicuous Member of Parliament, but he soon rose to the fore by virtue of his extraordinary oratorical powers and steely Puritanical fervor. Religious, economic, and constitutional issues converged, creating an explosive atmosphere as the King and Parliament contended for mastery. In the end, Parliament proved strong enough to strip the episcopy from the King and assume control of the army and navy. The King responded by gathering his faithful Cavaliers around him and raising an army of his own. The Parliament then made common cause with Scotland and marched against the King.

In these times, King Charles was off to war. In 1642 he raised his standard at Nottingham against the "roundheads" of the Parliamentary army, and England was thrust finally into the Civil War that had been brewing for so many years; it was a contest not only between the King and the Parliament but between High Church and Low Church, which is to say, the Puritans. In general, the tradesmen, the middle classes, and country squires such as Oliver Cromwell supported the Parliament while the nobility and the peasants supported King Charles. From the first, the Parliament had strong advantages: control of the ports of London, Hull, Bristol, and Plymouth; the backing of two thirds of the population; and access to three quarters of the nation's wealth. The people of London largely supported the Parliament and they built 22 forts and 18 miles of trenches to protect London from the Royalists. The Royalists in London had their homes confiscated to quarter the Parliamentary troops.

King Charles was a surprisingly adept military leader, enjoying several victories early on, although that was soon to change. Of course, King Charles never expected that this gentleman from Huntingdon would prove even more skillful in battle than he. War lasted four long years until finally the Parliamentary troops led by Oliver Cromwell and his New Model Army annihilated the Royalist troops at the

Battle of Naseby. The King became Cromwell's prisoner, escaped, was recaptured, and would soon meet his fate.

The war caused much suffering and deprivation. Not only were there thousands upon thousands of deaths and terrible injuries from battle, but the entire country was ravaged. Many suffered hardship, to a greater or lesser extent, as a result of the Civil War. The Chamberlens' practice decreased as well, but women will continue to have babies even in the worst of times.

The carnage went on despite the protestations of the people, including one from a surprising source. On September 22, 1646, a document was brought before Parliament by the midwives: *The Midwives' just Complaint, and divers others well-affected gentlewomen both in City and Country, shewing to the whole Christian World the just cause of their long-sufferings in these distracted times and their great fear of continuance of it.* It read in part as follows:

"We were formerly well paid and highly respected in our parishes for our great skill and our midnight industry, but now our art doth fail us, and little gettings have we in this age, barren of all natural joys, and only fruitful in bounty calamities. We desire, therefore, for the better propagation for our own benefit, and the general good of all women, wives may no longer spare their husbands to be devoured by the sword. We have with such horror and astonishment heard of Kenton, the Battle at Newbury, the Battle of Marston Moor, and the Battle of Naseby, wherein many worthy members and men of great ability were lost to the number of many thousand which doth make us humbly to complain that blood may not hereafter be shed in such manner, for many men hopeful to have begot a race of soldiers men were killed on a sudden, before they had performed anything to benefit the midwives." (Cellier 1643)

During these years, as Dr. Peter suffered great anguish for his friends and his country, he conceived a greater devotion to his God. He started to attend Saint Margaret's Church in Lothbury, where he joined the Anabaptist faith, believing that baptism should not be performed at birth but rather in adulthood when one is responsible for one's relationship to God. He also started to observe the Sabbath, a practice he accepted with little effort.

Chapter 36   King Charles I Execution – 1649

In 1646, King Charles surrendered to the Scots, who in short order turned him over to the English Parliamentary forces. In 1648, after his escape and recapture, he was accused of treason and was to be tried before a tribunal of 135 judges. Actually, only 68 of the judges showed up; 67 judges were unwilling to be associated with the trial of a royal monarch. On trial for his life, the King was charged as a "tyrant, traitor and murderer; and a public and implacable enemy to the Commonwealth of England." The King remained valiant and resolute. He eyed the judges with scorn, refused to take off his hat in respect for the judges, refused to acknowledge the authority of the tribunal, and even refused to enter a plea to the charges. The tribunal pronounced him guilty and sentenced him to death. The vote was 68 to 67 (nonvoting), and thus the fate of King Charles was decided by a single vote.

Three days later, on a bitterly cold January afternoon in 1649, King Charles was taken to the scaffold erected for the occasion in front of his newly constructed Banqueting Hall in Whitehall and executed. He had been allowed to take a walk in St James Park with his pet dog and eat a final meal of bread and wine. But the execution was delayed as the executioner refused to behead a king, as did other potential replacements. Finally, a man was engaged for £100s and was allowed to wear a mask to hide his identity.

An enormous crowd had assembled to witness this historical spectacle. In close to the scaffold, many soldiers swarmed to assure that the event would occur as planned. Wearing two shirts against the bitter cold so as not to shiver and appear afraid, Charles stood erect, hands and eyes skyward and prayed, then placed his head upon the block. The executioner tucked Charles' hair under his cap, and then the condemned king gave a signal. With one mighty blow the executioner severed the King's head from his body. The head was lifted up and displayed to the crowd while the body was put into a coffin covered with black velvet. Some people in the crowd, after paying, were allowed to go to the scaffold and dip their handkerchiefs in King Charles' blood, some to benefit from the perceived healing powers of a monarch and others as souvenirs of this great travesty (Encyclopedia Britannica 2002). The King had met a brave end and the Chamberlens lost a key supporter.

Chapter 37 A Voice in the Rhama

For years, Dr. Peter had been brooding over the way his attempt to incorporate the midwives had resulted in a judgment against him. He continued to hear of stories of birthing disasters that attested to the lack of training of midwives. His convictions to organize the midwives ran rampantly through his mind. He deeply resented the charge that he was taking advantage of patients and midwives and was less noble than he certainly believed he was. Peter had a tempest raging inside of him, still 13 years after his defeat at the hands of Shaw and Whipp, and it was stirred by comments of critics and enemies. On many occasions he set pen to paper to justify himself against this wrongful judgment. But whenever he attempted to write about it, he became enraged over the injustice heaped upon him. Finally, he was able to write, continuing until he had completed *A Voice in the Rhama: or, The Crie of Women and Children*, which was promptly sealed in a packet and sent by messenger to the printer. This, the most significant document created by Dr. Peter Chamberlen, was a hybrid of a plea for his midwifery incorporation scheme and a rant, eleven pages in all, considerably shortened and edited here for readability.

From *A Voice in the Rhama: or, The Crie of Women and Children* Echoed forth in the Compassions of Peter Chamberlen

Blood runs from the innocent veins of Women and Children as the fault of some uncontrolled female arbiters of Life and Death. My proposal to incorporate the midwives received the teste and approbation of those learned Columnes of our Faculty, Sir Theodore de Mayerne and Sir Matthew Lister. Its benefit being computed (over and above bettering of health and strength to Children and Parents) to the saving of above three thousand lives a year in and about London, besides the rest of England, and all other parts where the same Order may have been propagated.

Chamberlen obviously felt passionately about his plan to incorporate the midwives. His title *A voice in the Rama* is a Biblical allusion to Herod's slaughter of the innocents in Matthew 2:16-18, which in turn quotes from Jeremiah 31:15: "A voice was heard in Ramah, lamentation, and bitter weeping; Rahel [sic] weeping for her children refused to be comforted for her children, because they were not." (King James Version)

I was born in 1601 of honest parents who escaped the Parisian Massacres. I was educated in schools, universities and travels. In addition, I was taught Gallenical, Chemical, and surgical principles by my father and maternal and paternal family.

At the University I piddled in Chirurgery amongst my fellow-Pupils of Emmanuel College in Cambridge.

I did publick exercises in Heidelberg and Padua: and by age nineteen had received the Doctoral Robes of that Universitie, and wore my scarlet under the worthy Professor of Oxford Doctor Clayton, and the next year under the Doctor of the Chair in Cambridge.

I confesse, My Degree seemed big unto myself, and the pointings of the finger dyed my Cheeks with the reflection of my Robes. Yet I was led into Practice, which God blest with Gifts of Healing.

Then fame begot me envie, and secret enemies which mightily increased when my Father added to me the knowledge of Deliveries, and Cures of Women. Yet I was admitted to the fellowship of the College of London, and became subordinate unto my seniors. Thus I grew up to the Titles and Privileges

......

"I am no Pharisee, yet I justify my dealings with Men before God and Man......

First, my possessions are modest

Second, I served poor as rich

Third, I was never guilty of exaction

1.   I seldom bargained before performing a service

2.   I operated before I charged money

3.   I never arrested anyone for what was my due

4.   I never demanded full value for my services.

Many husbands, value his word at 500 but the danger to his wife not above 5. In summary, I am wholly tired out with the injuries.

I have served the Commonwealth 27 years, working night and day, not without hazard to my life. I have served the King and Queen by special command receiving only one reward and a Diamant-ring from her Majestie, but not any stipend at all from Either. If yet the Common-wealth may receive the benefit intended: for which I thus argue.

First, If my Wages and Titles, are justifiable, why may not the State as well resent a Proposition of Publick Good from me as from another? And if from me, then this is one Proposition I do yet recommend; *That some Order may be settled by the State for the Instruction and Civil Government of Midwives.*

Secondly, Though my Wayes and Dealings were not justifiable, yet why not so much good as I am able to do herein be accepted, and the evil that is found in me be restrained or punished?

Thirdly, Though I were the worst of men, so as not worthy to be named, yet why are not some more worthy Persons employed in this Proposition"

Dr. Peter wrote this emotional rant in 1647, some 13 years after the incorporation of midwifery had been rejected, describing his upbringing, education, and integrity as a foundation to challenge why the incorporation should not be adopted. According to him, the plan was needed and valid, but if he was not deemed worthy to implement the plan, then they should appoint someone else, so they could get on with the education and supervision of the midwives. This is a raw testimony to his devotion and passion for the cause. It is a strong argument against the position that he wanted to incorporate the midwives for profit.

Chapter 38   Dismissal from the College

1649 was not a good year for Peter Chamberlen. The loss of King Charles was tragic and in his opinion unnecessary. The King had the ability to abort this terrible tragedy but was too proud and stubborn to use it. The loss was heavy and penetrating, for Peter was a friend — if one can be that as a subject — and a confidante. He had enjoyed his times with the King and savored his relationship with him as advisor. In addition, the humiliation heaped on him by the Archbishop over the failed incorporation of the midwives continued to be almost unbearable. These problems weighed constantly on him, and so he did what he usually did in such circumstances: he turned his attention to several projects that were bursting in the recesses of his thought.

The first was a grand scheme to overcome poverty in England which demonstrated his sincere concern for the poor. Late in 1649 he completed work on *The Poor Man's Advocate or England's Samaritan*, which was a remarkable appeal to "the Supreme Authority in England, the High and Honourable House of Commons." His idea was to feed and clothe all the poor of England by making into "one common joynt stock" all debts due on public account, all mines "not wrought on at present," and the benefits of all manufactures, engines, inventions, and a host of other things. All thieves and robbers were to be received into a "house of labor," where they would work until they had paid off "double the damage they had done." Subsidiary aims were paying off all public debts in ten years and all the King's debts in twenty years, setting up a public bank, and erecting an academy for the education of youth (Aveling 1882, page 78).

The document outlining his scheme was ready. He ordered many copies from the printer and promptly distributed them to the Members of Parliament. But alas, with the King dead, the government was in such turmoil that his scheme never got a fair evaluation or the attention it deserved.

For a number of years, Dr. Peter had also been fascinated with the prospects for good health and hygiene that might be provided by public baths, such as those of Roman times. He had discussed this possibility extensively with King Charles and had even convinced him of their public health value, but now King Charles was gone.

He requested of the House of Lords an ordinance granting him a patent, for fourteen years, the monopoly of making baths and bath-stoves. This petition passed through the House of Lords to the House of Commons for consideration. He was optimistic because many members of Lords had commented to him on the wonderful prospects of the project. It may seem unusual that such a possibility existed at this time in history. But as explained in The Introductory to the United States Patent Office, during this unsuccessful attempt to establish a system of public baths Dr. Peter requested a patent for 14 years of exclusive ownership of the right to make and sell baths and bath-stoves for his public bath system. Although a patent had been issued as early as 1449, no further patents were issued for over a hundred years. Then April 26, 1552 a patent was issued to Henry Smyth to make Normandy glass.

Queen Elizabeth and her officers gave patents for inventions that would create financial benefits and technologic advances to the country. But the Queen also gave some favored courtiers or large contributors to the royal purse the exclusive privilege of selling salt, iron, paper, currants, sulfur etc. These abuses caused great upheaval and resulted in protests in Parliament. Queen Elizabeth gave a magnificent speech in Parliament in 1601 in which she professed ignorance of the problem this had caused and promised reform, promising the validity of her patent could be tested in court. King James had even more flagrant abuses causing Parliament to pass legislation.

169

In 1624, Parliament passed the Statute of Monopolies which made void all future grants of monopolies, but expressly excepted grants for 14 years or less for the sole working and making of any new manufacture within the realm. The statute became the basis for all subsequent patent grants in countries whose law is derived from English common law, whereby patents are distinguished from illegal monopolies. However, while the Statute of Monopolies limited the kinds of monopolies that the monarch could grant, it did nothing to give an inventor a right to a patent. An inventor still could get a patent only on the whim of the monarch. This short history of the origin of patents is pertinent to the Chamberlens as they did use the patent system for protection of their inventions, but it also gives some insight into the complexity of using this system for their secret instrument.

Now back to the fate of the patent for public baths and bath-stoves. Unfortunately, matters then took a turn for the worse, as the Commons referred his petition to the College of Physicians for an opinion. At this Dr. Peter despaired, for he knew the College would never give his plan a fair and just consideration. Predictably, the College replied testily that since "the Commons had not enjoined Dr. Chamberlen to attend the College concerning his design of baths, they could give no satisfactory answer therein (Aveling 1882, page 77)." When, on June 4, 1649, the College of Physicians declared itself formally opposed to his project, Peter became enraged and stopped attending its meetings. The College responded by sending him a formal summons demanding his attendance at meetings. At this time, Peter had such contempt for the College that rather than comply with the summons, he rented out his home and traveled to Amsterdam for a change of scene. Then, on November 23, 1649, his membership in the Royal College of Physicians was terminated by vote (Aveling 1882, page 77).

When he was informed of the College's action, he must have been awed by the power of the College and its ability to pervade one's life and attempt to snuff out one's career. But now there was no going back. He was done with the College for good and it with him. As for his public bath scheme, nothing more was ever heard of it.

These were troubling times for the Chamberlens. Political chaos ruled England following the execution of King Charles. Peter had lost his membership in the College, his public bath scheme was thwarted, he no longer had Court to attend; in short, he had nothing left to keep him in London. Hence he leased his house in London for six years and moved his family permanently to their country home, Woodham Mortimer Hall, in Maldon, Essex (Aveling 1882, page 77). Jane, probably, would have preferred to stay in London, for she loved opera, theatre, and the shops, and she had four decades' worth of friendships in the city. But she took on Woodham Mortimer Hall, with its 24 rooms, as a challenge, gradually transforming it into a warm and beautiful home. At the same time, they thrust themselves into the life of the town. In a short while, the number of people they considered close friends in Maldon became substantial.

Peter also quickly gathered around him a group of midwives who welcomed his services. With their help, he acquired many patients in Maldon, and soon his practice included travel to neighboring towns. He did not relish the long trips to these towns, but since he now had a carriage and a team of four horses, it was not a hardship. In truth, life in this setting would prove very satisfactory.

A new piece was added to the puzzle. This was the first time that the secret instrument had been used outside of the London area. And as we shall see this fact is significant as several versions of the forceps appear after Dr. Peter's death, in the Essex area.

Chapter 39   Mrs. Shaw's Dilemma

Though Peter's journeys to London were now less frequent, he traveled there in January, 1650, to see Gideon de Laune, who was enjoying his tenure as President of the Worshipful Society of Apothecaries. Gideon was well aware of the defeat Peter had suffered at the hands of Mrs. Shaw and Mrs. Whipp, so he hurriedly informed him of a recent event: On 4 January, at seven in the evening, 27 barrels of gunpowder, stored by a ship's chandler by the walls of All Hallows Barking by the Tower, exploded with a deafening force. Fifty houses, including the busy Rose Tavern, were destroyed; at least 67 people were killed (because of the force of the explosion, the precise number was difficult to ascertain). The wall of Hester Shaw's home was ripped off. Her son-in-law and grandchild had moved in with her. Her son-in-law Daniel Donne and three grandchildren, Thomas, Hester, and Elizabeth were killed in the blast. The mourning Hester Shaw had to find temporary lodging while the house was repaired. After the gunpowder explosion on her street, the constables found a hoard of money, over £3000, two bags of silver worth £100 each and quilted rolls of gold stashed under the floorboards of her damaged house. It caused quite a stir.

So Hester Shaw was not merely a poor working midwife with a cause after all. In 1650 Hester Shaw was described as a midwife of "Good esteem and quality." Clearly, Reverend Thomas Clendon found her formidable, and admitted that she was by many reputed religious, having her good education, and volubility of tongue and natural boldness, and confidence, attained some ability in prayer, and in speaking of matter in Religion.

During their absence, a great deal of property was taken from her home. Mrs. Shaw suffered severe financial setback, losing most of her belongings. She claimed to have lost £3000 without recompense. Curiously, her properties were subsequently found in the Reverend Clendon's house, he being the pastor at All Hallows Church. He refused to give them back to Hester Shaw and a fierce feud developed when she accused him of stealing. In turn, he openly decried her from the pulpit in several sermons. In 1653 Reverend Clendon complained of her allegations in his pamphlet *Justification, Justified*. She was a woman of wealth and determination. Not at all cowed by his denunciations, Mrs. Shaw continued feuding with Reverend Clendon, whom she was certain, had stolen her possessions. She was a bulldog who would never back down. Finally, in response to his attacks she published a pamphlet entitled *Mrs. Shaw's innocency restored, Mr. Clendon's calumny retorted.*

Hester Shaw was a fierce fighter and a literate woman, rare in her era in England. Evidence of her writing skills and determination are widely available.

"To the reader

A plaine relation of my suffering: by that miserable combustion, which happened in Tower-street through the unhappy firing of a great quantity of gun-powder, there the 4. of January 1650. Now printed that the world may see what just cause I had to complain of the injuries then done of me, and how little reason Mr. Clendon minister of that parish had (especially after three years times and more) to defame me in print as a malicious slanderer of him (though I had strong reason to suspect, I did never positively charge with any thing.) Yet he with as much malice as impertinency, hath inserted his vindication (as he calls it) into his epistle to the reader, put a sermon of his, lately printed entituled, Justification justified; wherein, however, he hath justified his doctrine, he hath condemned himself (as in reference to me) in the judgment of all rational persons." (Shaw 1653)

Hester Shaw was articulate and willing to stand up for her rights and defend her name. She was resourceful, forceful, and literate, and it is not surprising that her writing should be preserved in print as an example of an uncommon skill for women in 1653. Her skills and character shed new light on her ruthless battle with the Chamberlens in 1634.

Hester Shaw's fanatic attack on the Chamberlens over the incorporation of the midwives was predictable. She could see only the threat of men, and educated men at that, entering her trade and confiscating her livelihood. Indeed, she talked about the need for reform, but was so obsessed that she never addressed the real problems, the lack of education and standards. There was no education by the Bishop and inadequate visitation to see how midwives performed. The Bishop had a need for midwives for childbirth services for his 119 parishes, and licensing expanded and contracted according to the needs.

Mrs. Shaw had the ability to help overcome these deficiencies, yet all she could see was a threat to her livelihood. Both Mrs. Shaw and Mrs. Whipp were misguided. They missed an opportunity to be real reformers and leaders. Mrs. Whipp should be pitied most for she had the intellect and social position to accomplish desperately needed changes, but she just fell in line with Mrs. Shaw. They defeated Peter Chamberlen, but then they did nothing for the women of England—just something for themselves and midwifery as a trade. It was a sad and wasteful missed opportunity.

There was another note in newsprint: that Hester Shaw had mortally injured her patient when she forcefully tugged out what she mistakenly believed was her patient's placenta. It actually was her uterus. It came free and the patient bled to death.

Chapter 40   Maldon Cronies

Coffee was introduced to England from Turkey in 1651 and promptly became an enormous fad. Within a few years, many coffee houses had sprung up in London and in the surrounding areas. Maldon was no exception. In coffee houses throughout England people gathered to discuss the weather, the economy, and how The Dictator was ruining the country.

Oliver Cromwell had become Lord Protector of England in 1653. Though England was now a Commonwealth, in theory governed by a Council of State, it was in fact ruled by Cromwell as a virtual dictator. Parliament, led by a man with the remarkable name of Praise-God Barebone, became ultra-puritanical but had little real power. Cromwell himself claimed to promote religious tolerance, and to some extent that was true, for he allowed Jews to live in London for the first time since being expelled 350 years before by King Edward I. In truth, however, this tolerance did not extend to Catholics or Quakers, who were generally hated and harried. During his reign Cromwell brooked no opposition and ruthlessly put down revolts in Ireland and Scotland as well as the north of England. With none daring to challenge him, he became all-powerful, and his rule was in the end far more oppressive than that of any English king.

There was little anyone could do about it except complain. They would gather in Maldon on Wednesdays, minutes after the arrival of the London postal coach, bringing mail, but more importantly, tidbits of news from the City. From Maldon, they kept track of the political machinations in London. They thirsted for any reports, as radical changes were ravaging their country. Cromwell was making life unbearable for the people in England by his puritanical restrictions. Recently, The Dictator had a physician arrested for working on Sunday.

Meanwhile, Peter's practice was thriving, as he continued to perform deliveries with the aid of the special instrument, still safely secret. Since Maldon was just outside the jurisdiction of the College of Physicians, he was able to go about his business without their harassment. In addition, he busied himself with grand schemes that he believed would benefit mankind.

In 1658 Oliver Cromwell died. From his deathbed he appointed his obtuse son, Richard, who was so inept he was referred to as Tumble Down Dick. His mismanagement was so bad that the people pined for a return of royalty. At least then they knew what to expect and they had some degree of freedom. They clung to hope for it was rumored that Prince Charles was waiting in the wings.

Chapter 41   Hugh, Paul, and John

By 1658, three of Peter's sons were grown, educated, and using their family's secret instrument in the practice of midwifery in London, accumulating significant wealth. The oldest, and clearly Peter's favorite, was Hugh: scholarly, articulate, and possessing exquisite dexterity. Hugh was now 28 years of age, and his upbringing and education had been a perfect story of success. A facile student, he glided easily through his courses to gain his medical degree, and was licensed to practice midwifery by the Bishop of London. No writer has been able to find where he completed his university studies, but surely he did graduate from a university for he is addressed as Dr. Chamberlen in many documents but most importantly in The Royal Society ones. He quickly developed a busy and successful practice, numbering many members of Court and royalty among his patients. Paul was a different story. He was 23 and living on Great Suffolk, Haymarket, with his wife Mary and son, also named Paul. He was involved in more activities than just midwifery, which unfortunately later led to a major family embarrassment. Paul was a charlatan. It was he who had invented the notorious "Anodyne Necklace," which he then promoted and sold, claiming it could cure teething problems and relieve pain of women in childbirth, as well as fix just about any malady imaginable. The necklace, made with small beads, was sold for five shillings by a woman who lived above the Sugar Loaf, a confectioner's shop by Old Round Court near the Exchange in the Strand (Graham 1960). The humiliation Paul was bringing upon this great medical family is perhaps best illustrated by the following item, one of Paul's many advertisements in the Daily Journal:

> "When Dr. Chamberlen first recommended this Necklace to the World, the success of it was but in its Infancy. But upon the Doctor's Approbation of it, its

use began to grow so general in families that its Reputation soon became publickly known. Numbers of Children that were almost at Death's Door with Bleeding and Cutting their Teeth, receiving such Ease and Benefit after it was put on:

Insomuch that a vast many of these Incomparable Necklaces have of late years used by Dr. Chamberlen's advice (having testified himself his esteem of them to those who enquir'd to him about 'em) in Numbers of Families, who expresse their abundant Satisfaction the Use of them, and that they would not for anything but have had one of 'em for their Children. So that this Great Man's recommendation to its value, since he would never have advised the use of it to so many Parents for their Children as he did, unless he was well perswaded of its worth." (Aveling 1882, page 181)

Another advertisement for the necklace read:

"In and about London 12,000 children yearly die of their teeth, whereas out of great numbers who have only worn this necklace we do not know of one that has died. It naturally performs all these surprising effects from a secret harmony and sympathy in nature between this necklace and the human body." (Aveling 1882)

Below is a portrait of Dr. Peter Chamberlen taken from an engraving beneath which is "Paul Chamberlen, M.D., 1658." It is really the likeness of Dr. Peter Chamberlen, for at this date Paul would have been only 23 years old (Aveling 1882, page 30). Dr. Peter is wearing his periwig, which was the custom of the times, starting in France and promptly being adopted by the well-to-do in England. Peter has strong features, deep set eyes, a prominent nose, and a mouth up – turned at the corners, giving him a pleasant look.

Dr. Peter (Aveling 1882)

The youngest of the three, John, was just starting his midwifery career at this time, but he too was very busy. He already had earned a reputation for hard work and integrity, traits that had always been foremost in their family with the exception of Paul. Of course, John suffers by any comparison to Hugh who was an outstanding scholar and physician.

Nonetheless, John was reputed to be talented and honest.

All three of the sons were physicians who practiced midwifery in London. They all had the advantage of the secret instrument, but Hugh was the only one to excel to the level of becoming a national and international leader.

Chapter 42   Percival Willughby

Events in history are generally recorded as oral or written accounts. Certainly first person written accounts carry great credibility. The middle 1600s history of midwifery was greatly enhanced by the personal accounts of Dr. Percival Willughby, a man-midwife who had moved to London. He was a graduate of Oxford who had been practicing midwifery in Derby and surrounding areas. His experiences shed enormous light on the birthing process of the era and give us valuable stories. He wanted his daughter to have the opportunity to be educated in London, therefore, he had inquired of an apothecary friend living in the City if he knew of any practice opportunities in London. Likely, their apothecary contacted Peter Chamberlen's Uncle Gideon de Laune, whose connections in London as Head of the Apothecary's Guild were unsurpassed. Also likely is that Gideon subsequently helped Dr. Willughby get started and had introduced him to Hugh, Paul, and John who were contemporary man-midwives in the City. Of course, this is speculation, but it would be even more improbable that the men did not know each other in these small professional circles.

Born in 1596, Dr. Percival Willughby was the youngest son of Sir Percival Willughby and Lady Bridget Willughby of Nottinghamshire. He was educated at Eton and received a degree from Magdalene College, Oxford in 1620. He moved to London to be taught music, physic, and surgery by Mr. James Van Otten, barber-surgeon of London, who unfortunately died four years later.

Dr. Willughby returned to Derby as a physician, devoting the majority of his time to male-midwifery. As a scholar he kept extensive records and diaries of his practice and observations. Willughby's *Country Midwifes Opusculum* was not published until a century later in Leyden. His practice experiences included some gruesome tales of midwifery incompetence. He freely voiced his opinions, based on his extensive experience, and spoke of "high and lofty, conceited midwives, who yet will leave nothing to save their credits and cloak their ignorances." He described their use of "pothooks, sack-needles, silver spoons, thatchers' hooks, and knives to show their imagined skills" (Aveling 1872, page 88).

Dr. Willughby was a meticulous recorder of medical cases and facts and was the colleague of one of England's most esteemed scientists. His friend, the famous physician Dr. William Harvey, had visited his home in Derby. Dr. Harvey, a brilliant scientist, had preceded Dr. Peter at Padua and was now quite famous for discovering the circulation of blood in the body. He had also recently published *De Generatione Animalium,* in which he identified the role of female eggs in reproduction. He was very loyal to King Charles I and during the civil war in 1642 left London for Oxford with the royal court. His home was ransacked and many of his scientific papers were destroyed (Baskett 1997). Dr. William Harvey, perhaps the greatest medical research scientist in the history of England, was a close friend of Willughby, which gives great testimony to Dr. Willughby's credibility.

Dr. Willughby's practice accounts provided a rare opportunity to observe what midwifery conditions were like. "I was sent for from Stafford to come to a lady beyond Congerton, whose midwife had kept her several days in labor. I took my daughter with me. We traveled all night, and we were wet to our skins with much rain by the time we arrived at break of day. Sad to say, the lady had died, undelivered, before our coming. On seeing her, my daughter exclaimed, 'We should have ridden faster!' She never complained of the long journey or the brutal soaking we received. She surely has the right spirit for this trade" (Willughby 1972).

Dr. Willughby, who desired to educate the midwives in

the Derby and Stafford areas, soon found a similar need in London. He also related the story of a midwife in Threadneedle Street who recently had "caused several women perforce to hold her patient by the middle whilst that she with others pulled the child by the limbs one way, and the women her body another way" (Willughby 1972).

Willughby told of a midwife "who had her patient tossed in a blanket, hoping this violent motion would force the child out of her body" (Willughby 1972). Here Willughby elaborated his own philosophy: that it was best to leave natural labors to the safe conduct of "the invisible midwife, Dame Nature." "The midwife's duty in a natural birth is no more but to attend and wait on Nature and to receive the child, and (if need require) to help to fetch the afterbirth" (Willughby 1972). Willughby's views were certainly consistent with the Chamberlens': that the midwives should assist but not manipulate. The barber-surgeons or the physicians should provide the operative maneuvers for difficult deliveries. Of course Willughby was not aware of the Chamberlens' forceps other than by rumor or colleague's accounts at this time.

Willughby must have beamed with pride when he related one of his frequent stories of his daughter's tutelage and training, such as the following incident:

> "During her early midwifery experiences in London, I helped her as often as I could. But sometimes my being a man made it difficult, as when I accompanied her to assist in the labor of Sir Tennebs Evank's lady one day in 1658 in Middlesex. All that morning my daughter was much troubled because she feared that the baby was coming by the buttocks. About seven o'clock that evening as the labor approached, at my daughter's request and unknown to the lady, I crept into the chamber on my hands and knees to help with the exam. We then crept out, still unperceived by the lady. In my haste

and effort not to be seen, I concluded that the baby was coming head first, but my daughter confirmed the contrary, adding that if it turned out to be coming by the buttocks she knew how to manage the delivery. When she reported her finding to the husband, he behaved unhandsomely, uttering rude comments to my daughter that upset her. She could not be quieted until I crept a second time into the chamber and found that her assessment was correct. I urged her to bring down a foot, which she promptly did, but being disquieted with the fear of ensuing danger, she prayed me to carry on the rest of the delivery, which I was able to do unnoticed by the lady. To this day she does not know who delivered her...

Recently my daughter attended Mrs. Wolaston, a watchmaker's wife, who dwells by the old exchange on Threadneedle Street. In Mrs. Wolaston's first labor the previous year, the midwife did much tugging and struggling, but in the birth attended by my daughter, the woman had an easy and speedy delivery. That happy result, if I may say so, was due in no small part to my daughter's skills. The birth was indeed so effortless that the woman began to complain, thinking the child had not yet come. Discouraged and fearful, she said, 'Now I shall fall into the pains and sufferings of my first labor.' At that, my daughter smiled and asked what she meant, for her baby was already born. Mrs. Wolaston scarcely believed it, until she heard the child cry. Then she took my daughter's hand and said, 'Surely you have art in these fingers; otherwise I should not have been delivered so quickly and happily" (Willughby 1972).

His daughter had the skills, patience, and judgment to be a superb midwife. She was also fortunate to have an educated, well-trained physician midwife to guide her. Between the two they have given us a rare look into the state of midwifery in the mid 1600's England.

In the 2000 publication of *The Midwives of Seventeen-Century London*, Doreen Evenden states "Willughby became the highly visible author and midwifery "authority" and, although it has been commonly assumed that his daughter obtained her expertise from her father's instruction, there is every likelihood that the reverse is true, and his most valuable experience and training were gained through an association with his midwife daughter" (Evenden 2000). While her book is a positive contribution, I find this assertion unfounded and contrary to the recorded history.

One cannot ignore the historic value of a meticulously recorded diary (e.g., the Diary of Anne Frank gave us critical insight of what life was like for a Jewish girl in hiding from the Nazis in WWII Holland). This is a piece of history and one cannot change the story to accommodate a theory. The diaries of Pepys are a valuable portrayal of history. So too were the records of Dr. Willughby, Oxford graduate, physician, and careful recorder of medical history. The value of Willughby's writings is even greater because so few complete records are available from 17th century physicians. Willughby had practiced midwifery for many years in the Derby and Stafford areas before coming to London and he was clearly his daughter's instructor, as he says. How fortunate we are to have these observations of diarists when trying to evaluate a period of history. How much more we could have learned if Sarah de Laune or Jane Myddelton had kept diaries of this period?

Chapter 43   Renewal And Restoration – 1660

Tragically, in 1660 Jane passed away without warning. In the days after Jane's sudden death, Peter's friends from the *Maldon Brew* continued to look after him. Peter did not languish long as a widower, for a magnificent lady, Anne Harrison, soon entered his life. Anne lived in Maldon and had never married. They met quite by accident. Their wedding was not as formal as a London wedding, but it was much merrier. His *Maldon Brew* friends entertained them with endless toasts and stories well into the evening.

The Commonwealth ended in May, 1660, amidst general rejoicing, as Charles II returned to London in a bloodless revolution. Well, not quite bloodless. A few of the regicides were later tried and executed, and the bones of Oliver Cromwell were dug up and hung from the gallows at Tyburn for a day.

No sooner had Dr. Peter heard of the Restoration of the monarchy than he decided to petition his new King for reinstatement at Court. As he and his Uncle Peter had delivered Charles II in 1630 and he had succeeded Peter the Elder (his uncle) as Court midwife, he had no hesitation in writing this petition. He pointed out in his letter, "I was the only physician to their Majesties who had survived from "before the misrule"'" (Radcliffe 1989).

He sent the petition off by messenger and did not have to wait long. In 1661, in a surprisingly short time after petitioning, Peter Chamberlen was reappointed with the following reply:

> "Doctor Chamberlen, physician to Our Royal Father and Mother, ordinarily attending Our happy birth and there one of Our first servants, is Our servant and Physician-in-Ordinary. Which the duplicate thereof shall be sufficient to signify till Our letters patent

do more amply declare the same." (Aveling 1882)

He noted that King Charles II had discounted the Commonwealth's 11-year tenure, dating his reign from the death of his father. Peter Chamberlen was back in control.

In 1662 Hugh visited Peter and Anne in Maldon, accompanied by Dorothy Brett, daughter of Colonel Malcolm Brett of London. She was radiantly attractive and was a good match for Hugh in wit and social graces. She excelled in music, art, and domestic skills. Anne and Peter immediately took a liking to her. On May 28, 1663, Hugh married Dorothy Brett. The wedding took place in St. Paul's Cathedral in Covent Garden, with a reception at the home of Colonel Brett. After their wedding, Hugh and Dorothy settled in a court off Old Bailey and a year later became the parents of a son, whom they also named Hugh, undoubtedly after his grandfather Hugh Myddelton.

Chapter 44   The Great Plague - 1665

In April, 1665, a woman named Margaret Porteous started to feel dizzy and feverish, then vomited violently and fell weakly into bed. Two days later she died as London's first victim of the Great Plague. She lived in St. Giles, an overcrowded and poor section of the City where garbage and human waste were simply dumped on the streets. Filth and stench prevailed. Black rats flourished in the mounds of refuse that abounded in the streets and alleys. It was not surprising that the Plague started in this destitute neighborhood. As it spread, Londoners assumed that God had sent this scourge to punish the poor for their sins, and so they called it "the poor's plague." This disease proved to be more democratic, however, for it attacked the rich and poor alike.

Because of the overcrowding and poor sanitation throughout London, sickness was never uncommon. Consequently, it was not easy for a physician to spot the beginning of an epidemic. But during May, Hugh had begun to notice an increase in the number of ill patients. His first hint of the plague was that several of his ill patients died on the fourth or fifth day instead of gradually recovering. Initial symptoms of the disease were sweating, shivering, aching, and vomiting up blood. Fever, coughing, and coma were also seen. The victims then became covered with a red rash, followed by the appearance of boils called buboes. The disease was rapidly fatal.

As the plague ravaged the city, the wealthy departed to the country, where many had homes. Clergy, doctors, merchants, and City officials left in droves. The shops closed. The city streets became deserted as the people remained inside their homes for fear of exposure. Lacking any other source of help, they treated themselves with herbs and magic potions.

Hugh and his family still lived in the courtyard just off the Old Bailey. Like everyone else, he feared that the spread of the plague was putting his wife Dorothy and one year old son, Hugh Junior, in grave danger. He felt, however, that so many patients would need his help that he couldn't leave the City. Instead, he sent his father a message asking if Dorothy and their child could come to stay at Woodham Mortimer Hall. Dr. Peter, fearful for their safety, immediately dispatched a coach to fetch them. With its 24 rooms, there was plenty of room in their commodious home, and they were relieved and delighted to have them. As they settled in Maldon, Dorothy kept reiterating gruesome tales of the epidemic: countless sick, neighbors dying, and word of unbridled spread. She related how Hugh had returned from his patient rounds exhausted in both mind and body. It did not take Peter long to decide to go to London to help him.

Although no account exists of Peter joining his son in London, it probably occurred and this account is created.

* * *

As Peter entered the City, he was amazed that almost no one was about. The city was deserted, save for packs of wild dogs which roamed freely. On his way through the streets, he was stunned to discover masses of dead bodies that had been thrown out of windows. He stopped counting corpses when he got to fifty. Some were piled in heaps. London was never known for the sweet smell of its streets, but now the stench of decaying bodies was unbearable.

It was 10 o'clock at night when he arrived and found Hugh at home, dining alone with just two candles to light the room. Hugh appeared ghastly, worn out, and haggard. Shaking his head, he looked at his father and began to weep. "Father, I cannot believe you have come. You must go back. London is hell itself. Go back to the safety of Maldon."

But he must have known his father could not leave him there.

"Hugh, let me assure you that Dorothy and the children are secure in Maldon. Believe me, Anne will pamper them proper. I am here, Hugh, and I intend to remain because every other physician I know has abandoned London to protect his own hide. Only you have had the courage to stay, and I have come to stand with you. Say what they may about the Chamberlens! We are physicians, and with God's help we shall do what we can."

"Father, we shall. We shall do as you have taught me. And I am glad you are here."

"Where are your brothers?"

"Paul fled with his family to the country, and John took his family to his other house outside the City."

"I am so proud of you, my Son."

"And I of you, Father."

Hugh had stopped weeping. In fact, for just a moment, he flashed a smile. "Have some wine, bread, and cheese, Father. We must remain strong."

They ate and talked for a long while. Perhaps they should have tried to speak of old times or happy memories, but the horror consuming London dominated their thoughts. So instead they spoke of plague, corpses, and lost friends. They talked of old women conscripted to lay out the dead, and then throw the corpses out the windows. They spoke of mass graves. They talked of what needed to be done at sunrise to cope with marching death. In the fading candle glow, Peter was alarmed at how exhausted Hugh looked.

"I am happy you have come, Father. We must get some sleep, for we start at six."

"I will be ready to follow your lead."

At dawn, as they approached their first patient's home, a guard stepped forward, raising his stave to block their way. "Stand clear. You are forbidden to enter this house. See the red cross on the door? See the sign—Lord have mercy."

"I am Dr. Hugh Chamberlen. These are my patients. Stand aside. We will enter and treat."

"God have mercy," proclaimed the guard again. "I have seen no signs of life."

"Aside," ordered Hugh. "We are entering."

Hugh and Peter put on leather masks with huge pointed beaks. They must have looked foolish, but that was far from their minds. Their beaks were filled with cinnamon and other fragrant spices to ward off the foul smell and evil vapors. They took their bellows, filled with more spices, and aimed the nozzle inside the door. As Hugh began pumping, a large gray cloud of pungent-smelling air filled the room.

They cautiously opened the door and saw a dreadful sight: a mother and child lay dead on the floor, the mother clutching the child to her bosom. The child appeared but three, pale and covered with vomit. They advanced to the next room, finding the woman's husband alive but covered with vomit and excrement, lying helplessly on his cot. His sunken eyes suspiciously followed their approach. He tried to raise his arm but could not. He moved his mouth to speak but could not utter a sound. They set about giving him nourishment and a concoction of herbs. It was clear to them that he soon would suffer the fate of his wife and child. They could stay only a few minutes, as they had many other patients to visit. As they left the house and removed their masks, they found themselves gasping for fresh air and sweating profusely. Hugh instructed the guard to have the old women come to prepare the mother and child for the dead carts which went through the neighborhood every evening. Their sense of defeat was overwhelming: two dead and pitifully little to offer the miserable dying man.

They proceeded to the next home. No guards. No sign on the door. Maybe there was some hope. They went through their routine, fumigating, before entering. They slowly opened the door and saw no one. Moving cautiously to the back room, they found a woman holding her dead son, two other children crying at her side, and a man lying motionless on a cot.

"Help us," pleaded the woman. "Help us, Dr. Chamberlen. My child has died, my husband is weak and overcome with fever and cough. Must we all die? Get us out of here!"

"I am sorry, Mary. Truly sorry. But you cannot leave. You are quarantined. You must not leave the premises for forty days."

"But I will die. My children will die."

"Mary, you must obey the regulations. No one comes in. No one goes out for forty days," said Hugh resolutely. "You must listen very carefully. The quarantine is to protect you as well as other people. I realize you want to escape this area and go to a place not doomed by the plague, but these are iron rules. There are armed guards to enforce them." Hugh's voice cracked noticeably. The house had five people, one dead, one moribund, and a mother and two children still appearing well.

"The old women will arrive tonight to prepare your child's body for the dead cart," Hugh continued. "You must be brave and strong, Mary. Your husband will be buried in Black Heath. You cannot leave him in your home. We have treatment for you and your children. Keep up your nourishment. We will look in on you in two days. The Lord be with you."

The day continued on as a succession of tragic scenes. Exhausted, Peter found himself trailing Hugh and murmuring over and over "Lord have mercy." Hugh's posture was stooped and his voice raspy as, with darkness falling, they retired to his home, two beaten men.

* * *

Once it was clear that the plague was upon them, the Lord Mayor had ordered the gates of London closed. All visitors were forced to leave. Many other cities and towns throughout England followed suit, and they were not eager to receive refugees from London. Even letters from London were viewed as carrying disease and were burned or buried in the ground. The public, in desperation, looked to the King Charles II for support and guidance, but in July, the King departed for Salisbury, leaving the people on their own.

In London, the city officials were desperately trying to stop the fatal plague, but unfortunately nobody knew the cause. They tried many measures to stem the spread of the disease, but none worked and some made things worse. Believing that wild dogs and cats roaming the streets might be a cause, the Lord Mayor employed dog-catchers, who caught and destroyed more than 30,000 dogs and cats. Unfortunately, they had just destroyed the natural enemies of black rats, which now flourished freely. Heaps of raw garbage on the streets had fostered huge colonies of black rats. These rats were infested with fleas, and it was these fleas that carried the bacteria which caused the plague.

The plague had spread rapidly from St. Giles to the heart of the City itself, where the narrow streets, shops, and numerous warehouses provided the worst possible conditions. Mid July was very hot and even with the enormous exodus from London, the mortality rate soon rose to 1,000 per week. The streets were empty, two thirds of the shops were closed, and trade came to a standstill. Samuel Pepys' own physician, Dr. Burnett, became a victim. The worst was yet to come in late August and September, when Pepys wrote in his diary: "It is feared that the true number of dead this week is near 10,000; partly from the poor that cannot be taken notice of through the greatness of the number" (Pepys 1970).

In September, the Lord Mayor ordered the lighting of huge bonfires, hoping to purify the air and help rid the City of the plague. By late autumn, the death rate had decreased considerably. The shopkeepers slowly returned to the City.

By December, the worst was over and the shopkeepers took down their shutters. When the plague subsided, the searchers of the dead estimated that 70,000 people had perished (Pepys 1970). What is clear is that Hugh Chamberlen remained in London throughout the plague, endangering his life for the sake of his patients.

Hugh became involved in a plan to combat the plague and the Record Office holds papers written by him concerning ridding London of the plague (Aveling 1882, page 126).

"A few propositions concerning the Plague by H. C.

1. That 'tis very probable the plague will increase again this ensuing year.

2. That (in case ye plague would in few weeks of itself totally cease) yet it might be driven away in fewer.

3. That as there are secondary causes of it; so are there secondary remedies against it, promising as much reason, certainty and success, as most other sublunary undertakings.

4. That now is ye best time to endeavor it, both for saving greater expenses, certainty, & speed & safety.

5. That though £100,000 were expended upon it, yet (if successful) would ye advantages thence to his Majesty affayres and the Citty be a manifold requitall!

6. That greater sums have been expended upon designes of as little infallibility and no designe is infallible.

7. That is concerns every inhabitant of ye Citty, if not of ye whole Nation to contribute towards ye charge in a regular tax.

8. That freeing ye citty is a work very different from curing a patient. It being as well political as

Medicinal, & requiring ye Authority of ye Magistrates as well as ye skill of ye Phisitian." (Williamson 1992)

Chapter 45   The Great Fire - 1666

One could not title this chapter *The Fire* for, with wooden houses, open hearths, and sooty chimneys fires erupted daily around London. Fires were such a problem that the government admonished the citizens to rally with the firefighters to expunge any outbreaks. But, in September 1666, following a summer drought, in the setting of constant winds, a fire raged for five days ravishing the City; hence, the title *The Great Fire.*

The diarist Pepys provides a vivid account of the beginning of the fire: Sunday September 2 "Jane called us up, about three in the morning, to tell us of a great fire they saw in the City....By and by Jane comes and tells me that she hears above 300 houses have been burned down tonight....So I [went] down to the waterside and there saw a lamentable fire. Everybody endeavoring to remove their goods, and flinging into the river, or bringing them into lighters that lay off. Poor people staying in their houses as long as till the very fire touched them, and then running into boats or clambering from one pair of stair to another (Pepys 1970)." Below is the scene recreated as I imagine it.

* * *

Hugh was unusually busy in the months following the Plague year, for many of London's physicians had died or did not return. One Saturday evening after returning from seeing patients, he sat down to dinner with his family, all now safely restored to their home near the Old Bailey. There was such a chilly wind on this first day of September, 1666, that Hugh decided they would spend some time by the hearth before retiring. A quiet evening at home was rare, since his services were in such demand. They retired early and slept well.

Early the next morning the family was awakened by throngs of people racing through the streets shouting that London was on fire. Hugh stepped outside and grabbed one man by the arm.

"Fire? Where? Are you certain?"

"By all the Saints! It started near Pudding Lane, then spread to Fish Hill and extended southward and westward to the Thames. It is headed this way!" sputtered the man.

Hugh could smell the smoke and noted a strong wind that told him this was more than idle rumor. "How bad is it?" demanded Hugh of the man, who seemed intent on moving on to warn others.

"'Tis over 300 houses already burned. It's coming this way, I say!" cried the glassy-eyed man as he sped off. The streets were now filled with frightened and frantic people, coalescing in huddles to glean the news.

Hugh spotted a street guard and asked him what he knew. His news was the same: "I've been told the fire is out of control. The summer was hot and with no rain. The houses are like tinder. The wind is high. It's a disaster!"

Hugh ran indoors and summoned Dorothy. "Start packing up. You must take the family to Maldon, tomorrow morning, if not before. I have to see this for myself. For now, keep everyone inside. Lock the doors!"

Rushing back into the street, Hugh broke into a trot, running eastward. He knew he was on the right track, for the smoke got thicker as he ran. He hadn't gone more than a quarter mile before he could spot the flames. The air made him choke and gag, his eyes hurt and watered.

By noon on Sunday in Maldon, Peter Chamberlen had heard of a monstrous fire consuming London. Anne and Peter looked at each other and simultaneously began to shake their heads. First the Plague and now this. Surely it is God's wrath upon us in this year of the Devil's number.

"I'll send the carriage," Peter said. "We must fetch the family before it's too late."

Monday evening the family arrived, Dorothy, the children, but no Hugh. They were frightened but relieved to be in Maldon, once again their haven. As soon as the children were safely within the house, Peter pulled Dorothy aside.

"Dorothy, where is Hugh? Is he on his way? Is he safe?"

"What did you expect? He is your son. He has stayed behind because he insists his patients need him."

"Hugh, brave, stubborn Hugh," he muttered, shaking his head. "But there will be no one left in London to care for. They are all fleeing the inferno. Where are Paul and John and their families?" he asked.

"They were among the first out of town."

Once all were settled inside, they listened in anxious silence as Dorothy related the harrowing tale of the family's escape from London, extolling particularly the bravery of the carriage driver in fighting his way through the panicked mob. As Dorothy spoke, Peter felt an urgent desire to see Hugh, who was again staying behind and risking his life to help others. Anne and Dorothy comforted the children while Peter went out to speak to the coachman.

"How bad is it?' he asked.

"Like nothing you have ever seen, m'lord. I couldn't keep the team overnight at your son's house, for the fire was steadily advancing. I fetched the family at dawn and headed back to Maldon with four very tired horses. Had to stop five times to rest the team. There were people everywhere on the roads fleeing from London. A desperate scene."

"It must have been very frightening," he said.

"I was not scared for myself, but I feared mightily for your family. They were all brave as could be, though."

"Ahem...I am thinking about going to help my son in London. Could you make a run for it?"

"I have never known you to jest, m'lord. Are you serious?" he retorted, turning to face Peter squarely.

"Very serious," Peter asserted.

"Well, this team would not survive a run tomorrow, but we could borrow another team from the Blue Boar, or wait till early Wednesday."

"Find a team. We shall leave at dawn."

Peter turned and entered the house, trying to devise how he would break the news to the women.

Their trip to London was some 45 miles, a distance Peter estimated they could cover in six hours with fresh horses and a little luck. It took them 12 hours because of the multitudes exiting the City. The highways were strewn with lost and castoff belongings of people fleeing for safety. As they neared the areas north of the City, they saw many thousands in various states of despair lying by the roadside with heaps of possessions. As they went through Islington, their carriage came to an impasse many times as throngs of people headed to a field where they were erecting tents for shelter. The unbroken stream of humanity stretched all the way back to the City. The majority were on foot, but others were using every form of conveyance imaginable. Closer to London, just outside Highgate, they saw another tent city of desperate, displaced families. It seemed like half the population of London was camping out in these fields.

They learned that their best way to enter the City was toward the west, for the fire was still raging in east London. They inched along, taking in the misery of the wretched people fleeing their homes. Since they were returning while everyone else was fleeing the City, they were able to wedge their way through without very many trying to stop them or beg for a ride.

They rode through a burned-out area to approach Blackfriars. Peter was initially disoriented, for all the familiar landmarks were leveled. London smelled of dank soot, and smoke still rose from the charred ruins. Knowing beforehand that it would be difficult to breathe, they had brought wet cloths, which they now placed over their mouths and noses. The air was so laden with ash that little sunlight could reach the City. It was almost as dark as night. All surfaces were gritty underfoot. Black and gray building skeletons lurked everywhere.

Miraculously for Hugh, the fire had destroyed neither his home nor that of his neighbors, for two houses on each side; however, the area smelled so badly of smoke and ashes that it was not habitable. When they arrived, Peter was startled to see Hugh's house still standing with its neighbors, like a sooty silhouette, an island in the wasteland of burned-out London. They were not at his home five minutes before a guard arrived to question their intentions. When he found out Peter was Hugh's father, he told them they could find Hugh at Nigel Baskin Lawson's home just a half hour's ride away. Then they spotted a note Hugh had nailed to his door giving directions. Somehow Nigel had found Hugh and invited him to stay in his home in Knightsbridge to the west of London, which the fire had spared. This was a great favor for Hugh because most people had to leave the city for lack of housing.

When they reached Nigel's home, Hugh and Nigel raced out to greet Peter. Hugh looked surprisingly hale for a man who had been through such an ordeal. They embraced warmly as Peter assured him that his family was safe in Maldon.

Peter sent the carriage back to Maldon with instructions to tell Dorothy that Hugh was safe and looked well. He gave the coachman some coins for his good work.

Then they sat in Nigel's dining room buzzing almost exclusively about the inferno that had leveled London.

"You, Hugh, are most fortunate," Peter said. "Your home still stands. Quite sooty, but not a complete loss like the others."

"Fortunate indeed," added Nigel. "The destruction of property is unlike anything ever seen before in England. But so far, Peter, we have heard of only a few people dying."

"Yes, unlike the time of the Black Death," said Hugh. "At least people could flee the fire."

Peter suddenly realized why they were so sanguine amidst this total devastation to the east end of London. People had lost their homes but not their lives. It was tragic indeed, but there was still hope for them. Not so with the Plague, which left some 70,000 Londoners dead.

Hugh related the beginning of the exodus.

"Sunday afternoon and all day Monday everyone was attempting to flee. The roads were clogged with carts, buggies, wheelbarrows, or whatever one could find with wheels. People were flocking down to the Thames and standing on the wharves until boats could pick them up and carry them to safety. They were in constant fear as they moved from wharf to wharf trying to keep ahead of the advancing fire, but almost everyone managed to escape.

"The firefighters fought bravely, but with the high winds it was a losing battle," Hugh continued. "The people are supposed to pitch in and help the guards and the firefighters when fires break out, but in this case the conflagration was so overwhelming that they just grabbed whatever possessions they could and ran."

"Not everyone ran," said Hugh. "Our King was riding through the streets surveying the damage when he came upon firefighters tearing down a house to create a fire break. He at once leapt from his carriage, grabbed an axe, and joined in the work. It was a rare sight to see a King wielding an axe, and happily Hugh was there to see it. He was fierce. Then he gave the firefighters some coins from his purse as a reward. Won back some support of the people with those heroics, he did."

The next day the fire was under control. It appeared that the valiant firefighters could bring it to an end just west of the City. Indeed, the fire halted finally on Cock Lane. That evening, surrounded as they were by devastation, they joined with the people of the neighborhood in a joyous celebration.

* * *

Once the fire was out, the King issued proclamations to help the homeless, providing tents and food, and ordered soldiers to clear the debris. In addition, money started to pour in daily to the Lord Mayor and the Anglican Church from all over England to provide relief for the homeless. Tent cities arose in fields south of the City, and in Moorfields and Islington, north of the City, where upwards of 100,000 destitute people were sheltered.

The Great Fire reduced 400 acres of London to ashes over four days; 13,200 houses and 400 streets were destroyed; 41 of the 56 company halls of the City of London were consumed. St. Paul's Cathedral was destroyed, as were most of the government buildings of the City of London. Almost all of the 97 parish churches were burned to the ground. With all of this destruction, it was miraculous that only nine lives were lost. The devastating fire also had one beneficial result: it eradicated all of the black rats and ended the lingering presence of the Plague.

The rebuilding of London was an excuse for Peter to make frequent visits to see Hugh and his family. This should not be surprising, for, as Peter admitted, Hugh was his favorite offspring. They saw eye to eye on all matters, save the fate of the secret instrument.

Activity in the City was frenetic. A "fire court" was set up to settle claims of lands. Most new buildings were erected on the burned-out foundations of the old. All construction, by royal decree, had to be of brick or stone to lessen the risk of future fires. Within a year, the City's trade had resumed its vitality.

Hugh and Peter enjoyed recounting their many adventures during the Great Plague and the Great Fire. It was also a time when Peter could share with his son stories about Jane and his new wife, Anne, man to man.

In these years, in addition to practicing his profession, Peter continued to work on inventions. From the time of his boyhood reveries on Blackfriars jetty, he had always been fascinated with harnessing the wind to propel ships. So, after working with small wooden models, he designed and obtained a patent for a rig that would enable mariners to sail within two points of the wind, if not full against it.

In April, 1666, Dr. Peter traveled to Holland, putting all of his enthusiasm and energy into a new project from which he expected to reap great gains. He had so much faith in it that he applied to many countries for patents to secure the advantage of any profits for himself and his family. From Amsterdam, he wrote to Hugh to ask him to secure the patent for the invention in England, but in this Hugh failed him (Aveling 1882, page 90-93). Gradually, Peter lost his enthusiasm for this project.

He returned to England and continued to visit with Hugh every few months. Hugh's apparent readiness to sell the family secret probably was a matter of conflict with his father. Yet this will always remain a mystery. Dr. Peter seemed unable to convince him that if the family secret were to be divulged, it should be given to the medical community to benefit all mankind. Their family had preserved it all these years mostly for their own gain, to be sure, but also to see that it would be used properly and generously. Had they not often charged nothing for their services when the patient was too poor to pay?

One evening, Hugh again brought up selling the secret instrument and announced that he had arranged to go to Paris to see what he could get for it. What follows is clearly set forth in documents.

203

Chapter 46   Professor Mauriceau

It is not surprising that, by 1670, the fame of the Chamberlens had spread throughout Europe. Hugh, always very enterprising, saw an opportunity to use the family fame and secret to make some money. He had heard the story of the French "royal accoucheur," Dr. Clement, and of his prowess and good fortune. In 1670, King Louis XIV had summoned 22-year-old Jules Clement, a well-known male midwife, to attend his mistress, the Marquise de Montespan, who was in labor. Clement was required to enter the bedchamber blindfolded. He performed the delivery with aplomb and was rewarded by the king, who bestowed on him the title accoucheur. He was subsequently called to deliver the Queen of Spain and all of the Spanish princesses. He also attended several other members of the French royal family. The favor of King Louis had made it quite fashionable in Paris to employ a male midwife (Radcliffe 1989, page 31).

Hugh wrote Dr. Clement to propose a demonstration of the family secret technique and mentioned a possible sale for 20,000 crowns. Clement did not accept the offer, but he told another famous French physician, Professor François Mauriceau, about it (Radcliffe 1989, page 31).

Mauriceau was an accomplished male midwife. He recognized the Chamberlens as skilled practitioners of the art of midwifery, though he did not believe there was anyone on earth who knew more than he in this area. Nevertheless, a burning curiosity prompted Mauriceau to invite Hugh to come to Paris and demonstrate his secret technique to extract a baby without hooks.

On August 19th, 1670, Professor Mauriceau was asked to see a tiny woman on the fourth day of her labor. Her waters had drained away on the first day, and her contractions had stopped. Professor Mauriceau recommended bleeding her and, if that did not work, giving her an infusion of two drachma of senna to restart her pains. On examining her, he was unable to introduce his hand, which by his own account was quite small, because the pelvic passage was so close and the sacral bone so curved on the inside. As a result, he concluded that it would be quite impossible to deliver this tiny woman. When he declared this impossibility to his

Francois Mauriceau (artist unknown)

assistants, they immediately advised that he bring the child out by Cesarean operation. He chided his assistants that this operation was always fatal to the mother and was used only when the mother had died with a live baby in her belly. Despite the Professor's great experience and skill in accomplishing deliveries, he had nothing more to offer her.

That same day Hugh set out from London for Paris, starting with a two-day carriage ride on the Dover Road. Drawing on the wisdom of his grandfather, he engaged a driver-protector for the journey. Crossing the English Channel and landing in Calais, the two travelers continued by carriage, hoping to arrive in Paris at the appointed time. They stayed overnight in a comfortable inn outside Paris that proved quite suitable. At dawn the next morning, Hugh gathered his belongings and the large carved wooden box and headed by carriage for l'Hôtel Dieu.

Arriving on Île de la Cité in the middle of the Seine, Hugh was impressed to see the imposing structure of the famous hospital occupying a whole city block, adjoining the square of the Cathedral of Notre Dame. L'Hôtel Dieu rose several stories, its many wings casting a huge shadow in the early morning sun. To Hugh, it appeared colossal.

Hugh had heard much about l'Hôtel Dieu and the expertise of its physicians. Now here he was, standing in front of it. He recalled that l'Hôtel Dieu had been built as a monastic foundation and run as a charity by the Catholic Church. Currently administered by the City of Paris, it was large enough to house 1,000 patients with all manner of diseases. Even so, it was notoriously overcrowded and commonly had a census of 1,500. Nine of the wards contained medical, cancer, consumption, and trauma patients. One ward, Salle Saint Joseph, was devoted to diseases of women and obstetrical patients.

As a religious foundation, the hospital accepted patients to the maternity ward with no questions asked. Their names were recorded in the central office, but thereafter never divulged. Most of the babies delivered were illegitimate and were subsequently abandoned by their mothers. At this time, of the 1,500 babies delivered annually, about 1,300 were adopted or more often sent to a foundling home. The girls would be raised until they were placed as domestics and the boys were sent to the army.

Hugh knew of many famous surgeons of the legendary l'Hôtel Dieu. Of these, the most renowned was Ambroise Paré, born in Laval, France of Huguenot parents. He had come to l'Hôtel Dieu in 1533. Lacking the classical education necessary to qualify for the College of St. Come, the powerful College of Surgeons, he trained to be a less prestigious barber-surgeon. Paré made up for his lack of Latin and membership in the French College of Surgeons by gaining extensive surgical experience, performing all the operations that were beneath the dignity of the surgeons. He left l'Hôtel Dieu after three years, becoming attached to an army field commander and making an excellent living.

At the end of a campaign in Turin, he returned to Paris, passed his examinations, married, and bought his wife a home. He then enrolled in an anatomy class at the University of Paris, taught by the young Sylvius, who had so bitterly disappointed Vesalius at Padua. Paré was very happy in his work, for he loved living in Paris and he excelled at anatomy. Over the next 20 years, he was called back several times into the army, where he gained an excellent reputation for humane treatment of the wounded, serving both officers and common soldiers.

Paré became the leading European surgeon of his time and was the author of several outstanding books on surgical anatomy. He also had an extensive knowledge of midwifery and held a strong view against the practice of rupturing the membranes.

In 1549, he described how to manage certain situations, such as transverse lie of the fetus, shoulder presentation of the fetus, and brisk bleeding before the baby is delivered. In the technique called internal podalic version, the operator should reach into the birth canal and displace the baby upward, then grasp both of its feet and gently pull downward to deliver the baby as a breech. He angered his surgeon colleagues by writing this chapter in French, for it was their tradition to treat such subjects only in Latin, the language of scholarship.

It was by this technique that Jacques Guillemeau subsequently saved Paré's daughters life. Here are excerpts from Paré's description: "and then let him put his hand gently into mouth of the womb having first made it gentle and slippery with much oil; and when his hand is in let find out the form and situation of the child...and turn that his feet may come forwards...and when he hath them both out, let him join them together, and so by little and little let draw the whole body from the womb" (Baskett 1997, page 172-3).

Another surgeon at l'Hôtel Dieu deserves mention: Louyse Bourgeois, a star pupil of Paré, and the first woman to write a textbook of midwifery for midwives. In 1601, she became the flamboyant and outspoken midwife to Queen Maria de Medici, wife of the French King Henry IV, delivering her six children, the last of whom was Queen Henrietta Maria, wife of King Charles I of England, whose man-midwife was Hugh's father.

Dr. Bourgeois wrote the first book on obstetrics by a midwife. "Most of the obstetrics advice in the book was based on the teachings of Guillemeau and Paré. She did however have her own quaint remedies, including one for arm presentation. In such cases she advised the placing of the infant's hand in a pan of cold water to stimulate the withdrawal back into the uterus. She does acknowledge that if the child is too feeble, the accoucheur may have to replace the arm and do an internal version and breech extraction (Baskett 1997, page 25-6).

We are very fortunate to have Professor Mauriceau's own account of Hugh Chamberlen's visit to Hotel Dieux which was initially circulated among his colleagues and subsequently published. Therefore, it is possible to reconstruct the occasion.

* * *

And so, in a state of high expectation and supreme confidence about the prospects of his visit to Dr. Mauriceau, Hugh arrived at l'Hôtel Dieu an hour before his appointment. Wandering into a men's ward and entering almost unnoticed because of the confusion of many people coming and going, he was awestruck by the sight. The ward was arranged to hold 30 to 40 beds by forming three rows, one on each of the sidewalls, and one down the center of the long narrow room. All of the beds had posts and canopies with side curtains. Most of the curtains were open and tied up to the bedposts so that one could look through the entire ward and see almost every patient. Each bed was occupied by at least two and as many as four patients. They were laying head-to-toe, with an additional person lying crosswise at the end of the bed. Many of the patients had one or two family members standing or sitting near the bed. They were the sole source of feeding, toileting, or any pretense at cleansing. Next to many beds was a patient sitting on the floor, leaning against the side of the bed, waiting for one of the patients to leave or die. Commonly, when a patient died, it was many hours until the overburdened porters would arrive to remove the body. Hence, the live patients were forced to share the bed with each other and a corpse.

The smell was overwhelming. It was a stench of overcrowding, of bodily aromas, and frank decay. The constant background sound of moaning from miserable patients was unnerving as well. Up and down the aisles passed a constant stream of relatives and friends visiting the patients. Additionally, there were hawkers and peddlers and even beggars. They were joined by visitors to Paris, who commonly strolled through the wards merely to see one of the city's famous sites. This was a public spectacle. The scene was unlike anything Hugh had ever witnessed or imagined, worse than any alms-house he had seen in London. Yet this was the famous l'Hôtel Dieu that boasted reports of marvelous treatments and cures.

When the time for his appointment arrived, Hugh, somewhat dazed, staggered out of the ward with the large carved wooden box securely under his arm. He found Professor Mauriceau's office and entered.

Hugh greeted Professor Mauriceau and complimented him on his reputation as an accomplished accoucheur.

"I too have heard many amazing things about your art of midwifery and the successes of your father and your family. I had the pleasure of meeting your father at a meeting in Paris five years ago. He is a marvelous man. Very impressive." said Mauriceau.

"Thank you very much. Father sends his respects," replied Hugh.

"Now to the matter at hand," said Mauriceau.

Mauriceau continued: "I am happy you have come on this particular day because I have a 38-year-old patient having her first baby whom I would like you to see. She had 8 days of ruptured membranes with no labor. During this time, the midwives made her walk every two hours but had no success in starting her labor. Then they shook her, but still could induce only minimal contractions. Last night, they gave her a large dose of senna, causing a generous emptying of her bowels. She is now finally in very active labor. I consider her delivery to be a fair test of your secret instrument. If you can deliver her successfully, I will be interested in learning more about your technique and possibly purchasing it."

Hugh pondered the situation for a moment, and then replied.

"I accept your proposal, m'sieur. I shall need only eight minutes for the delivery, but I will require complete privacy during the time I prepare for my technique. Once I am prepared, I will allow six of your accoucheurs to be present and then the room will be locked during the delivery."

"Bon," responded Mauriceau, as he ushered Hugh to the doorway of the ward, Salle Saint Joseph. A midwife, who was examining the abdomen of Hugh's soon-to-be patient, spotted them and promptly came over to meet them. Professor Mauriceau indicated that she should introduce Hugh to the patient and assist him in whatever he needed. Hugh then politely dispatched Professor Mauriceau, repeating. "I shall require eight minutes."

Mauriceau departed.

Hugh glanced over the ward and noted that there were some 40 beds, all containing women, most with three or four occupants. Most of the women were waiting to go into labor. Once they were in active labor, they were moved to a bed shared by only one other person, or, if lucky, they got a bed to themselves. Such was the case with his patient; she occupied the bed herself. As Hugh approached the bed, he was appalled to see that his patient was a dwarf. Now he could find nothing lucky about this patient.

Since women in labor in Paris were used to having male midwives, Hugh did not need to spend much time trying to assure the patient that she would be safe and comfortable with a male attendant. He indicated to the midwife that the patient should walk to the chaffoy for her delivery.

It was not surprising that Professor Mauriceau would present him with a difficult delivery to demonstrate the secret technique. Even so, Hugh probably had not expected anything like this. This was going to be as challenging a test as he could be given. He estimated the patient who was lying in bed would measure about 4 feet 2 inches in height. Her tiny frame would present difficulties enough, but to Hugh's dismay, he also spotted the tell-tale bowing of her legs that is commonly seen with rickets, a condition caused by vitamin D deficiency, in which the long bones are weak, distorted, and curved. Such a disease could seriously distort the spine and pelvic architecture as well, making it difficult, or impossible, for a baby to pass through the birth canal. In this case, as he judged the woman was three weeks early, Hugh hoped the baby might not be too large and that the bones of its head might still be flexible enough to fit through the birth canal, making the delivery feasible.

As the patient walked, aided by the midwife, to the chaffoy, Hugh was shocked to observe that she was even shorter than he had estimated. She could not be any taller than 3 feet 11 inches. Once the woman was in the chaffoy, Hugh instructed the midwife to have her lie down on the bed. In l'Hôtel Dieu, a standard-size bed was used for deliveries, the birthing chair having been abandoned many years ago. The custom was to use a bed-sheet to cover the patient. This could serve Hugh's purposes well. He would be able to perform his delivery under the concealment of the sheet. The secret would be safe, thought Hugh, even though there would be many experienced observers, all anxious to catch a glimpse of the secret instrument.

Hugh surveyed the room. It was approximately 20 by 25 feet in area and had no windows. However, it had a skylight that, with the morning sun, was providing good illumination. There was ample room for the six observers who would later be allowed to attend.

When his patient lay flat, directly on her back, Hugh's concerns deepened. Her uterus jutted straight forward, protruding far enough that he judged the baby to be very big. Furthermore, the top of the woman's uterus extended all the way up to her chest. The delivery of a rachitic dwarf with a large baby was an overwhelming, perhaps, impossible challenge. Many people already knew about this test of his skills, however, so Hugh realized he must not fail. He stripped off the patient's gown and observed her total body configuration, getting her to rotate to the right and to the left. Nature had been cruel to this woman: not only were her legs bowed but her spine and pelvis were also markedly deformed. As if this weren't enough bad luck, her baby appeared to be too large for her pelvis.

Hugh recalled three rachitic women in labor whom he and his father had encountered in London. All were relatively short, but none were dwarfs. In one case, the baby was already dead when they were called and in another it died during the delivery, even though the secret instrument had been employed. The third was delivered with difficulty with the aid of secret instrument and seemed to do reasonably well, though he had recently heard that this child subsequently had some difficulty with talking and walking. But this case was different; in his entire experience, he had never encountered a dwarf with severe rickets.

He spoke to the mother in French, saying that this delivery would be very difficult and would require her full cooperation. He warned that, at times, it would be painful, maybe excruciatingly painful. The mother was extremely weak, and her eyes were sunken and hollow. When asked if she understood, she just gave an affirmative nod.

Hugh instructed the midwife to give the tiny woman a grain of opium, then to help him get her positioned on her back at the bottom of the bed. Her knees were spread apart about 14 inches. Then her feet were brought close to her buttocks and were placed about 9 inches apart. She seemed not to object to the positioning, for she was already exhausted and welcomed any sign of renewed effort to solve her problem. Indeed, she knew two dwarf friends who had died in childbirth, so she was very aware of the risks and resigned to a dismal outcome.

Hugh gave the midwife two choices: she could leave the room and wait outside or she could stay to help prepare but would be forever sworn to secrecy. She had heard of the Chamberlens' prowess and quickly chose the latter option.

After hearing her decision, Hugh opened the wooden box and carefully laid the secret instrument next to the patient on the bed under the sheet, trying his best to prevent the midwife from seeing it.

"We are ready," he said. "Fetch the six observers and allow them to stay on the far side of the room. Then lock the doors."

When all were assembled and the door was locked, Hugh said, "Bon, we shall proceed," and, looking at the midwife, added, "Now pull her knees up and outward."

Hugh now attempted to insert the secret instrument into the birth canal and was pleased to find that this approach seemed to be working. For the first time in 30 minutes, he began to feel that he just might have a chance of success. He told the midwife to push on the top of the uterus as he pulled downward and outward, but the baby did not budge. Then he readjusted the instrument, set his foot firmly against the bottom of the bed, and gave a maximal pull downward and outward. As he did so, he slipped off balance, causing the instrument to slide off the baby's head and come all the way out of the vagina, landing on the bed but still safely concealed by the sheet. At the same time Hugh himself lurched backward and fell off his stool, landing on his buttocks on the floor. The six accoucheurs simultaneously managed to stifle their laughter.

Hugh picked himself up and restarted the procedure. This time he instructed the midwife to stand at the patient's head with her hands under the patient's armpits. "Pull up hard now!" he commanded, as he again pulled down and outward with the secret instrument.

This time he lurched backward but did not fall as the instrument again came out of the vagina. A steady flow of bright red blood was now emanating from the vagina, staining the bed sheet. Every few minutes, the red circle increased in size. Hugh attempted this technique five more times, and the bleeding became more persistent. When

Hugh told the midwife he would have two more tries, the midwife whispered, "The mother is barely responsive. I want to leave because I am afraid your secret instrument will kill the mother."

By this time Hugh feared the baby was dead. Could I have failed? He decided to consult with Professor Mauriceau. He carefully returned the secret instrument to the wooden box that he had inserted under the sheet. Then he left the room, wooden box under his arm, the midwife remaining in attendance, and the onlookers actively murmuring to each other.

Professor Mauriceau was unimpressed.

"C'est vrai. It is true that this was a challenging case. But you claimed that you would need only 8 minutes and you have been trying for over three hours. I believe the secret technique has failed the trial."

"But this was a most difficult and unusual test of the secret," protested Hugh. "Indeed, this is the most difficult delivery I have ever encountered."

"You should have expected no less," countered Mauriceau. "The trial is over. I am not interested in buying the secret. I admire your skills and your ingenuity, but the case is closed."

Unfortunately, the baby was already dead, and after a long night with a weak pulse, the mother died the next day, undelivered. Hugh was distraught and humiliated over his failure; even worse, his patient and her baby had died. Hugh was worried that his father would learn of his failure even before he got back to London to tell him.

* * *

After Hugh had departed, Professor Mauriceau himself performed a postmortem dissection and found extensive lacerations of the uterus and genitals. He concluded that the mother had died as a result of infection and a massive internal hemorrhage. When he later published the autopsy findings, he cited the large hands of Dr. Chamberlen as one of the factors that had contributed to the mother's death, adding to Hugh's humiliation.

Hugh was not to come away from Paris empty-handed, however, for Professor Mauriceau had given him his book, *Traité des maladies des femmes grosses et de celles qui sont accouchées [Diseases of Women Pregnant or in Labor]*, to translate into English, with the prospect of handsome royalties. Hugh returned to London with the book and his carved wooden box. The secret therein was still safe, if somewhat diminished in reputation.

Chapter 47   The Book

After returning to London, Hugh immersed himself in translating Mauriceau's book, so he could ameliorate the torment of his Paris fiasco. The therapy was effective, for he had a power of concentration and enormous determination. Everyday Hugh arose at dawn and worked on his translation of *Diseases of Women*. The endeavor was easy for he had maintained fluency in the language of his heritage. The undertaking required a little more than a year. His only interruptions were pleas from midwives to help with difficult deliveries, which proved to be enjoyable diversions.

Hugh's version of the text, which he entitled *The Accomlish't Midwife*, was published in 1672 and was very well received by physicians and midwives throughout England and eventually the continent. In the Preface, Hugh made reference to the family secret, providing direct evidence of the use of the secret forceps:

> "My father, brothers and my self (tho' none else in Europe as I know) have, by God's blessing and our industry, attain'd to and long practis'd a way to deliver women in this case (obstructed labour) without any prejudice to them or their infants: tho' all others (being oblig'd for want of such an expedient to use the common way) do and must endanger, if not destroy one or both with hooks... I will now take leave to offer an apology for not publishing the secret I mention we have to extract children without hooks when other artists use them, viz., there being my father and two brothers living that practice this art. I cannot esteem it my own to dispose of, nor publish it without injury to them." (Dunn 1999)

The book was highly sought after, so Hugh was well rewarded for his efforts. Rumors indicated that he made upwards of £40,000, for it seems he had full rights to the gains of the book in England, so he did not have to share them with Professor Mauriceau.

The Chamberlens were disappointed to learn that Mauriceau planned to publish the case history of Hugh's failure for the entire medical world to read. In a draft circulated privately and passed on to Peter by a physician acquaintance returning from Paris, Professor Mauriceau described it thus:

"On the 19th of August 1670, I saw a tiny woman aged 38 years who had been in labour of her first child for eight days. The waters had drained away on the first day that she began to have pains, with hardly any dilatation of the womb. Having remained in this state up to the fourth day, I was asked for my opinion by the midwife, to whom I advised that she be bled, and that in this case the bleeding did not produce the effect that one might hope for, to make her take an infusion of two drachma of senna, to provoke pains which had ceased. However, for all of that she was not delivered, and her infant which came headfirst, but the face upwards (occipito-posterior), stayed always at the same place, without advancing in the passage; this woman who was so very small had such a narrow passage, and the bones which made it so close and near one another, and the sacral bone so curved on the inside, that it was quite impossible for me to introduce my hand to deliver her, although my hand is small enough....I declared the impossibility of delivering this woman to all the assistants, who being well persuaded of this, desired me to bring out the child by the Caesarean operation; which I would not do, knowing that it is always very certainly mortal to the mother.

But after I had left the woman in this condition...there came very soon an English doctor, named Chamberlen, who was there in Paris, and who from father to son, made a normal profession of midwifery in England in the City of London, where he had acquired the highest reputation in this Art. The doctor seeing the woman in the state I have described, and having learned that I had not found any possible way of delivering her, declared himself astonished that I had not completed the delivery, I whom he said, and fully believed to be the cleverest man of my profession in Paris. Notwithstanding this, he promised to deliver her in less than eight minutes, (un demi-quart d'heure), whatever difficulty he found there; to do this, he soon got to work, and instead of eight minutes, he worked hard for more than three full hours, without stopping except to take breath. But having uselessly spent all of his strength, as well as all his industry, and seeing that the poor woman was near death at his hands, he was constrained to give up, and confessed that he could not complete it, as I rightly declared. This poor woman died with her child in her belly twenty-four hours after the extreme violence with which he had treated her." (Mauriceau 1752)

Chapter 48   Transitions

As time passed, the embarrassment of the disaster of the failed delivery in Paris seemed to bother Hugh less. The celebrity he achieved from the book certainly helped him put the incident behind him. Had his attempted sale of the instrument eroded his friendship with his father? Of course it had not. They realized that they were alike in their desire to excel and prosper but accepted that they had very divergent opinions on how best to do so. Peter was extremely fond of Hugh and had discussed with his son his intention to propose that Hugh succeed him as the royal accoucheur.

In 1672 John Hinton, in the King's retinue of physicians, was retiring and had just been knighted for his midwifery services. The time seemed right for a petition to King Charles II to advance Hugh's career. Peter moved swiftly to bring Hugh to Court, where he was able to recommend him as his successor, "to supply the defects of my aged attendance" (Graham 1960, page 191). Peter had every confidence that Hugh would be accepted, since the Chamberlens had such a distinguished record of service; indeed, they had attended three Stuart kings and their queens for close to a century.

One year later, in 1673, Hugh was named Physician-in-Ordinary to King Charles II. Peter Chamberlen was overjoyed, for this appointment firmly established Hugh as the leading man-midwife in England. Hugh was a bit more complacent. He had been receiving honors and recognition in other pursuits, so he did not appear as ecstatic as his father about his advancement. Moreover, having by now put the Paris fiasco out of mind, he had fully regained his natural confidence and perhaps even thought such recognition his due.

In Maldon, Peter and Anne were content with their life in the quiet countryside. Peter's first family with Jane was healthy, his sons were doing well in their practices, and there was reason to believe they would enjoy the Chamberlen good health and longevity. But Peter and Anne's family suffered a tragic situation. They had five children, three sons and two daughters, their son Hope being the first-born. By the time Peter passed away in 1683, Hope was the only survivor of the five. Four children were lost in childhood, a situation not too rare in those days before discovery of immunizations against infectious diseases. Childhood illnesses like typhoid, diphtheria, and cholera commonly took the lives of young family members. Unfortunately, little is known of the circumstances of Peter and Anne's losses. With his first wife he had 13 children and all thrived and enjoyed longevity. Contrast this with the family of Peter and Anne, and one sees an 80 percent childhood death rate. This leaves one to speculate whether there could have been a genetic condition like Rhesus immunization, or hemolytic disease of the newborn, where their firstborn (Hope) escapes the problem but the subsequent pregnancies can be progressively more affected, resulting in fetal death, death at birth, or death soon thereafter. Perhaps there was a history of congenital heart disease or a metabolic syndrome. Of course, in the absence of such causes the losses could have been due to infectious diseases and accidents. Whatever the cause, this must have been an overwhelming tragedy for this couple to bear. As devastating as this may have been, Hope was active and in good health at the time Peter died in 1683, as Hope was the one who arranged for the funeral and the engraved monument to his father. Indeed, he was the one who eventually sold Woodham Mortimer Hall to the wine merchants' guild some 32 years later.

Over the next several years, having turned some of his practice over to younger colleagues, Peter directed his ingenuity to conceiving devices that he believed would benefit the populace as well as his purse. One was a way of writing and printing English whereby better to represent to the eye the sounds heard by the ear. Adoption of such a system, he was sure, would make it easier for people throughout the kingdom to learn to read and write. He received from King Charles II a grant for the full benefits of this invention for fourteen years. Translated to current times, Peter was granted a 14 year patent conferring sole rights to his invention. The preamble of the US Patent Office history refers to the Chamberlen's patents as evidence of such inventor protection many centuries ago.

At this time, Peter also received a patent for a scheme to propel carriages in the same manner as ships. The principles were the same. The power of the wind was harnessed in a sail to provide forward propulsion. The difference was that carriages, being confined to the roadways and trackways, were much more limited than ships in their maneuverability. Besides, in the city, houses and buildings tended to block the wind and make it otherwise unpredictable. The prospects for the success of this invention were hence only middling.

In addition, he became deeply involved in religious questions that culminated in his most prescient idea: to bring about the Union of the Christian Churches. This was not a whim or sudden urge; it was rather a burning drive or compulsion to engender peace and harmony among God-fearing men. He had considered various ways to accomplish this end, testing each eventuality, and he finally felt confident that he had a workable scheme. He wrote up his plan in the simplest form and decided it was time to present it to Archbishop Sheldon.

Archbishop Gilbert Sheldon became Bishop of London in 1660 and in 1663 was enthroned as Archbishop of Canterbury, a position of enormous responsibility and power. From Lambeth Palace he ruled over the southern two-thirds of England, presiding over 30 bishops, was active in matters of the Navy and Oxford University, reformed the

Book of Common Prayer, and found time to serve on the King's Privy Council.

Of course, the Archbishop of Canterbury was not easy to see, even for a man of Peter's exalted station. By this time Dr. Peter had been a minister in Mill Road Church and had been physician-in-ordinary to King Charles II. But to the Archbishop, of course, Dr. Peter was a nonconformist, and by reputation somewhat of a religious zealot. He had to rely on letters and regular visits to his office, where he was treated cordially and allowed to leave messages with an assistant for the Archbishop.

As for his proposal, even he must admit that it was not modest, but in his judgment and fervor, he believed it was possible. In a letter to Archbishop Sheldon, he described it thus:

"My Lord:

In plain English (my Lord) Who more fit and capable that Your Grace to invite the Pope, Cardinals & all the Heads of Jesuits, Sorbonists, Jansonists, Augustins, Dominicans, and Franciscans, together with the Chief of the Lutherans, Calvinists, Socinians, Arminians , and whoever else are for Paul Apollo or Cephas: to meet in Post Paper: and Conspire. Not how far they can Differ & Quarrel Each other but how Close they can Unite, and become all of Christ And to that purpose Each to Declare that Chief & Impartial Rule that they are persuaded in Conscience to stand by....

Your Grace's
Most humble, and faithful
Though unknown servant
2 October 1673 PETER CHAMBERLEN" (Aveling 1882)

When he did not receive an answer, he penned another letter to Archbishop Sheldon:

"My Lord:

I durst not trouble your Grace with much things for your Great Favour, nor with Excuse for want of my Aged visits. But having my thoughts employed in a Business of the Largest volume, for the Peace of All Christendom: I thought it most fit to present the Management & Honour of it to your Grace: that, being approbed, Your Wisdom & Authority might engage All Bishops & clergy of England, with His Magesties Leave & Approbation. While His most Christian Magesty engagest those of France and Our English Cardinal Norfolk engageth the Pope & Rest of the Cardinals, to Unite All Churches of Europe into a Reformation, by Advising about the Angels coming to the greatly Beloved Prophet Daniel concerning the little Crownd Horn's Change of Times & Lawes Which being discovered What Times & Laws those are. Good Council may be taken from those Angels that appeared to the Beloved Disciple John, To Blott out & Escape the Mark of the Beast: & Return to the Keeping of the Lawes of God, & the Faith of Jesus, as celebrated by the Angels. I shall now wayt the signifying of your pleasure to

Your Grace's

Most humble servant

PETER CHAMBERLEN" (Aveling 1882)

After several such letters proposing the Union of the Churches to Archbishop Sheldon, most unanswered, he eventually decided to try his fortune with the new Archbishop Sancroft. In 1677 Sancroft had succeeded Sheldon as Archbishop of Canterbury. He was very busy presiding over 30 bishops and was deeply involved in a pressing project, rebuilding St. Paul's Cathedral after the

Great Fire. By now Dr. Chamberlen's persistence was very well known to Lambeth Palace due to letters and requests for visits. He respectfully wrote to Archbishop Sancroft as follows:

"My Lord:

I most humbly thank Your Grace for presenting my Letter to His Majesty & for returning it to me, upon His Refusal. Which necessarily obligeth me to beg pardon for so great a Trouble. Tis my Province to do His Magesty Service, and He not know it: at His coming into the world & into His Kingdoms. Bene Facere & Male Audire Christianum est. However, if Your Grace vouchsafe to influence my endeavor at Universal Reconsiliation I shall not think my Labor lost. For I know, the hansom improving of what the Angel Declared to the Prophet Daniel (chap 7.25) may do wonders, though begun by

My Lord
Your Grace's
Most humble
Christian servant
29 October 1681 PETER CHAMBERLEN"

(Aveling 1882)

It is not known whether an informal face-to-face meeting with Archbishop Sancroft ever took place. If it did, the likely message would have been: your plan is good, perhaps even has a chance of succeeding. However, the time is not yet right. Go home and pray that the opposite persuasions move closer. After many years, these exertions took their toll on Dr. Peter, but after all, he was 80 years old and by now perhaps a little eccentric.

Of interest to the story of the forceps is that we can see a man whose scope is perhaps a little misguided but clearly enormous and altruistic. Peter wanted the unification of the churches as a phenomenon that would benefit all Christians in the world. This is not a man who is self-serving or greedy. He had nothing to gain personally from this quest. In his earlier scheme *The Poor Man's Advocate or England's Samaritan* he wanted to create a social system to help the poor in which all people of England would benefit. This is what makes this story so intriguing. If this man was so interested in helping mankind, why were the forceps still kept a secret after eight decades, and for how long would it remain so?

Chapter 49   Hugh Excels

With age, Peter Chamberlen's frame had become creaky, his memory less sure, and his eyes dimmer. The wheel turned and his time was almost done. The Chamberlen prowess and reputation rested with Hugh. His book had taken its place as the standard midwifery text wherever English was spoken and read. He was renowned everywhere as a scholar who had vision and courage. And now he had received an even greater honor. You can imagine Peter's pleasure and pride when, in 1681, Hugh was elected a Fellow of The Royal Society of London for Improving Natural Knowledge ("Royal Society" for short). That his son had achieved such a distinguished level of recognition was so important to him that he was immediately able to bury his unrest over their philosophical differences.

The Royal Society of London for Improving Natural Knowledge was the world's first and most prestigious scientific society. It had its origin when 12 men met following a lecture by astronomer and architect Christopher Wren at Gresham College, Oxford University. They decided to set up a college promoting Physico-Mathematical Experimental Learning. Actually this initiative had precursor groups meetings in London and Gresham College. In 1638 the group split into the Oxford Society and the London Society due to travel distances. In 1662 they petitioned and received from King Charles II a royal charter for the Royal Society of London. In 1663 the King signed a second royal charter making it the Royal Society of London for Improving Natural Knowledge.

The founding fellows were mainly in mathematics, medicine, or science. Fellows were elected for life by a vote of their peers. In Hugh's case, when elected in 1681, those peers were men such as Christopher Wren, initially a mathematician, astronomer, physiologist, microscopist and later an architect; Robert Boyle, chemist and physicist; Isaac

Newton, mathematician and physicist; and Samuel Pepys, diarist. They met regularly for lectures, as Robert Hooke's demonstration of glass expanding and contracting with heat and cold, and William Croone's experiment of transfusing blood between dogs. They debated positions as the purpose of breathing was to refrigerate the blood, then, demonstrated that the inspired air had some interaction with the blood. They formed committees to study critical issues. Since the society comprised less than 200 fellows, it is clear that Hugh would have known all of these virtuosi. They were the most brilliant lights of London and perhaps the world.

Over the years the Royal Society continued to grow in importance and membership. Benjamin Franklin, discoverer of electricity, became a member during his residence in London. After residing in several locations, the Royal Society moved to its current home at Carlton House Terrace in 1967.

Though it had royal patronage nearly from the start, the Royal Society has always remained a voluntary organization, independent of the British state. In 1945 it started to admit women. Today it has approximately 1300 fellows and 130 foreign members. The Royal Society serves as scientific advisor to the British government and receives grants-in-aid. It is also the UK's Academy of Sciences and finances research fellowships and research grants. The Society's role includes providing independent advice on matters of concern, administering large sums of public money for grants supporting innovative research, fostering international scientific cooperation, and encouraging better communication between scientists and the public. Imagine the enormous achievement it was for Hugh Chamberlen to be elected to this world renowned Society in 1681, and how proud his father must have been.

Chapter 50   One Man's Decision

By early 1680, Dr. Peter had already lost most of his teeth (one of the items found with the cache of forceps was a tooth wrapped in paper with the writing *"my husband's last tooth"*). He had outlived his life expectancy by decades. As a medical man, he would have realized that death could strike anytime. He made a will: "In the name of God Amen. The ffowerth day of May Anno Domini One Thousand Six Hundred Eighty and One, And in the Three and thirtieth years of the Raigne of our Soveraigne Lord King Charles the Second of England. I Peter Chamberlen Doctor of Physick his Majesties first and eldest Phsician in ordinary of his Royal Person being weake of Body But of good and perfect mind and memory (All praise be given to God) Doe make and ordaine the my last Will and Testament in manner following" (Aveling 1882, page 121). Although he stated he was weak he made it perfectly clear that his mind was quite sharp. He was alert and making sound decisions and he even composed a poem to be inscribed on his tomb as he proceeded to get his affairs in order.

There was unfinished business, for the forceps still remained a family secret. For generations all of the family had prospered from the use of this device. By now most barber surgeons and physicians realized that the Chamberlen family had some manner of delivery instrument. Indeed, Hugh had referred to the forceps in the 17th chapter of the second edition of his translation of Mauriceau's book, then the major midwifery book in the English language. . . "my author justifies the fastning Hooks in the Head of a Child that comes right, and yet because of some Difficulty or Disproportion cannot pass;... But I can neither approve of that Practice, nor those Delays; because my Father, Brothers, and my Self (tho none else in Europe as I know) have, by God's Blessing and our Industry, attained to, and long practiced a way to deliver Women in this Case, without any Prejudice to them or their Infants; tho all others (being obliged, for want of such an Expedient, to use the Common Way) do, and must endanger, if not destroy one or both with Hooks."

In the 27th chapter Hugh wrote "I will now take leave to offer Apology for not publishing the Secret I mention we have to extract Children without Hooks, where other Artists use them, viz. there being my Father and two Brothers living, that practice this Art, I cannot esteem it my own to dispose of nor publish it without Injury to them, and think I have not been unserviceable to my Country, although I do but inform them that the fore mentioned three Persons of our Family and my Self, can serve them in these Extremities, with greater Safety than others."

Hugh's position on the secret instrument was clear: he wanted to profit by selling the instrument. In 1670 Hugh had attempted to sell the secret to the French government for 20,000 crowns, and failed. The secret continued to benefit the family and their patients, but not the profession, the people of England, or the world.

Dr. Peter had a strong history of creative genius and knew that their invention could be protected for 14 years with a patent, a mechanism he was familiar with, and quite proficient in obtaining. He was certainly aware that once a patent was obtained the protection would last only a decade and a half, but at this juncture the forceps had already been kept a family secret for over eight decades. Clearly, the decision to keep the instrument a family secret was calculated and deliberate. To his dying days he was committed to keep the secret, for he asked his wife Anne to hide the forceps, which she did with obvious deliberation: the trap door in the third floor of Woodham Mortimer Hall was cleverly and skillfully crafted to secret the instruments. Peter died in 1683 but the Bible that was discovered with the cache of instruments bears a manuscript date of 1695, so we can surmise that the hiding place was constructed, or was added to, sometime after Dr. Peter's death. The important facts are that Dr. Peter wanted the forceps hidden and Anne dutifully carried out his wish.

Peter had a history of charity and concern for the poor. He had travelled abroad and was concerned with international issues. He was a man with a strong set of moral principles and by this time had been a minister for three decades. What then could have gone into his decision not to share the secret with the world? He had three sons currently employing the instruments. He still had grandsons who would become male midwives who could use the forceps to prosper in practice. Indeed, Hugh Junior was in his last year of Cambridge and would follow a successful career as a man midwife. Most of the need for these instruments could have been satisfied in and around London, at least, by employing the Chamberlen family to aid in problem deliveries. No such instruments were known at the time in England or the Continent. So it is fair to say that that the Chamberlen family possessed the means to transform the practice of midwifery by promulgating information concerning the forceps to barber-surgeons and physicians, but this did not appear to be a major priority. The concept of utility to the rest of the world was not part of his agenda.

Chapter 51   Dr. Peter's Final Days

At age 82, Peter had love for all of his children and, in his own case, that takes a great deal of love, for with his two wives, he had 18. Jane and he were truly blessed, as they had eleven boys and two girls, and remarkably for that era, all grew up without any being lost to illness or accidents.

Anne and he were not as lucky with their five children. Their oldest son, Hope, was stalwart, kind, intellectual, and a natural leader; but each of their younger children died prematurely. With each passing the pain mounted. Parents simply should not have to bury one child, much less four.

Concerning all of his children, each was unique and precious. With few exceptions they were thoroughly honest, had strong personal convictions, and knew what they wanted to do with their lives. Peter had always taught his children (when he could) to give back to society for the many blessings that they have received. Of course, first they were to give God His due, but then they were to be grateful and return some of their largesse to mankind, which would please the Lord. On balance, he thought, his children grew up to be worthy and charitable, adding more mystery to why the forceps secret was not given to the medical profession. There were times when he believed that Hugh and Paul listened the least to his heeding, but they were good men and he was proud to be their father.

His wives were a source of inspiration and comfort beyond anything he deserved or could ever describe. Each created a home and a family life that he cherished. Even beyond that, they both had the spirit to make life exciting and each day a welcome challenge. He had been a fortunate man. He had been truly blessed.

He had asked Anne to hide the secret instruments on the top floor of their home after his death. He must have made this decision with many misgivings, for he truly understood the life-saving value of the instruments and knew if given to all physicians and barber-surgeons many more people might benefit from their invention.

As he grew older and weaker, he realized that he would soon have an appointment with His Maker. He prayed and thanked Him for his blessings. He hoped his Good Lord knew that he was never mad, perhaps too passionate in his poor attempts to serve Him, but never insane as some had charged. He hoped God would know that he was a dedicated minister.

A few months earlier, he realized he was dying, so he set about to compose a poem for his tombstone. He would probably cite only a few lines, for he feared he had inherited the trait of verbosity from his Grandpapa William de Laune, and he did not want to overdo things.

To tell his learning and his life to men
Enough is said, by here lies Chamberlen;
Death my last sleep, to ease my careful head,
The grave my hardest, but my easiest bed

Hope made all of the funeral arrangements. He arranged to have an engraved tomb for his father and on it was inscribed:

Here lyes ye body of Doctor Peter Chamberlen, who was born on the 8th of May, 1601, and dyed on the 22nd of December, 1683, being aged 82 years 7 months and 14 days. He had two wives, and ye first Jane Myddelton, had 11 sons and 2 daughters, and amongst them 45 grand-children and 8 great-grandchildren (whereof were living at his death 3 sons viz. Hugh, Paul, and John and his 2 daughters and 20 grandchildren and 6 great grandchildren.) By ye second, Anne Harrison, had 3 sons and 2 daughters, whereof only Hope was living at his death, who hath erected this monument in memory of his father.

The said Peter Chamberlen took ye degree of Doctor of Physick in several Universities, both at home and abroad and lived such above three score years, being physician in ordinary to three Kings and Queens of England, viz. King James and Queen Anne, King Charles ye First and Queen Mary, King Charles ye Second and Queen Catherine, and also to some foreign Princes, having traveled to most parts of Europe, and speaking most of the languages. As for his religion, he was a Christian, keeping ye Commandments of God and faith of Jesus, being baptized about ye year 1648 and keeping ye 7th day for ye Sabbath for about 32 years." (Aveling 1882, page 1220)

Although Dr. Peter passed away the secret instrument was still very much alive.

Chapter 52   The Ethics of the Secret

The Chamberlens undoubtedly invented the obstetrical forceps. Discovery of the cache of instruments belongings to Dr. Peter, the documents of Mauriceau, and the writings of the Chamberlens provide direct evidence. The indirect evidence was the extraordinary demand for their services, and the questioning of the College of Physicians of Dr. Peter over the incorporation of the midwives. "What makes you say that you could deliver a difficult labor better than any other member of the college?" That line of questioning clearly indicated that they believed he had a secret instrument and were eager to learn it.

There is little doubt that Peter the Elder was the inventor, most likely with the collaboration of his father William Chamberlen. Although the absolute timing is not known, the best evidence places it in the year 1595, the year after Peter the Younger moved to London and a year before William retired to London only to die shortly thereafter. Consider if you will: how else could one explain how Peter the Elder—an immigrant without a university degree— could arrive in London and have such meteoric success? He arrived in 1597, passed the exam for the Barber–Surgeons Company, established a celebrated practice, and was appointed Physician-in-Ordinary to King James I and Queen Anne in 1604.

By the time of Dr. Chamberlen's death the Chamberlen family had the secret forceps for approximately eight decades. The instrument was a closely guarded secret which allowed their practice to flourish, bringing them wealth and fame. As immigrants moving to England with little money, they must have felt justified in not sharing this secret for it was their ticket to restoring the family wealth lost fleeing Paris. During this era there was not a strong precedent for giving away medical discoveries. Most physicians had their secret potions. "Balsalm of bats" was a favorite of Dr.

Theodore Turquet de Mayerne, the king's physician (MacDonald 1952). The ingredients consisted of three snakes cut into pieces, twelve bats, two puppies, a pound of earthworms washed in white wine, common oil, malago sack, and bay leaves. The whole disgusting brew is then boiled up and strained, and the marrow of stag and ox bones added to it along with "honey of dogs" nettles. This was applied to the backbone to cure a whole array of illnesses, few of which were actually afflictions of the back (Cook 2001).

Even the famed physician William Harvey had his secret formulas. Edmund Chapman, who in 1733 first wrote of the use of forceps, admitted to having a secret technique of delivering with a fillet. The sheer drama of keeping the instrument secret surely made the Chamberlens' daily practices most challenging. Each delivery tested their knowledge and skills as well as their cunning in protecting the secret. No doubt the practice also provided some humorous situations. As their goal of secrecy became permanently ingrained in their daily practices, it is easy to understand how the concept of sharing the discovery with mankind faded into the background.

The opinions of their colleagues were not altruistic. As an immigrant family recently arrived in London, they experienced extraordinary success. Perhaps other barber-surgeons even felt some pride in the fact that two of their members were so successful using some mysterious but effective instrument. But that is pure conjecture, for the Barber-Surgeon Company was constantly harassing them for not attending meetings and much of this could have stemmed from jealousy. Certainly, their success had not gone unnoticed by their barber-surgeon colleagues, for there were many attempts to discover the secret or steal the instrument itself.

The Chamberlens' success initially caused little notice by the College of Physicians, for their members rarely performed surgical procedures and had little or nothing to do with childbirth. What eventually irked the College of Physicians was the Chamberlens' constant transgressions by prescribing and practicing Physik. As Peter the Elder and Dr. Peter were regular attendees at Court and became the male midwifes of three reigns of Kings and their Queens, the members of the College of Physicians no doubt were jealous, and this was reflected in their subsequent judgments and decisions concerning the Chamberlens' midwifery practices.

Until Hugh failed to sell the instrument to Professor Mauriceau, it was unlikely that the physicians on the Continent had any awareness of the secret, other than hearing some tales of these famous barber-surgeons. With the frequency of ships sailing between London and the Continent there was likely a constant flow of news, both accurate and not.

Their patients seemed to be aware that an instrument was being used, but they neither saw nor heard anything that gave them a clue to its nature. Certainly they knew friends who lost babies or died in childbirth and realized the secret instrument had saved them from that fate. The midwife would have explained the importance of a barber-surgeon's skills in convincing the father to permit her to engage these men. Then there was the fee paid to the Chamberlens, high but not excessive for their level of training, expertise, and use of the secret instrument, and of course, in instances of the poor there sometimes was no fee at all.

Incredibly, the forceps were in active use and kept a family secret for over a century. The decision to keep this a family secret instead of obtaining a patent seems to be sound when considered from the prospective of gaining wealth through the invention. The secret was to endure five generations, whereas a patent only lasted 14 years, after which time it enters the public domain. At this time patents were granted by the King, and Dr. Chamberlen had already obtained several. Therefore, keeping this as a family secret was deliberate and financially sound, but was surely only in the Chamberlens' self-interest.

Chapter 53   What Could Have Been?

What could have happened if other major scientific inventions were kept as family secrets and not shared with other physicians? One can only speculate on the stifling of progress in medicine if the stethoscope, invented in 1816, had been kept as a family secret for 130 years. In early medical practice, physicians placed their ears directly on the patient's chest to listen to the heart beat and sounds of breathing, a procedure called auscultation. In this setting, imagine examining patients who hadn't bathed in months. Only a small number of homes had running water, and all water had to be heated by the hearth. Educated, wealthy persons may have washed their hands and faces daily, but a bath would have occurred weekly at best. Furthermore, there was risk of infectious disease. Some diseases, such as tuberculosis, were highly contagious, but the germ theory had not been developed yet. Robert Koch didn't identify *Mycobacterium tuberculosis* until 1882. Obviously direct auscultation had some serious risks.

In 1816, a young French physician, Rene Theophile Hyacinthe Laennec, embarrassed when faced with examining a young woman's chest, rolled 24 sheets of paper into a tube, placed one end on her chest and the other to his ear, discovering he could hear surprisingly well. An expert in wood turning, he soon made a cylindrical instrument he subsequently called a stethoscope.

By 1817 Laennec published a paper describing examining the chest with a stethoscope, which he termed "mediate" auscultation versus the traditional practice of placing one's ear on the chest, "immediate" auscultation. The Laennec stethoscope was a 1.5 by 12-inch wooden, tubular structure with an ear-piece on one end and a chest piece on the other. Laennec quickly shared his discovery with his medical colleagues, describing in his text auscultatory signs we still use today, some two centuries later. Bruits, rales, and bronchophony are chest sounds, well known to all modern day medical students. Physicians promptly learned these heart and lung sounds in order to diagnose and treat disease introducing a whole new era in medicine. Laennec died in 1826 shortly following publication of his second edition of his text. Following his death physicians made modifications to his monaural stethoscope, the most notable being the Priorry scope, approximately 7 inches in length. By 1850's physicians made major changes as they introduced binaural stethoscopes, flexible tubing, chest diaphragms, and many modifications continuing up to the present day.

Ironically, the disease that killed Laennec was tuberculosis, which was mainly diagnosed by the stethoscope until the invention of the chest x-ray by Wilhelm Konrad von Rontgen around the turn of the century. The stethoscope was invaluable in diagnosis and treatment of pneumonia, heart disease, and many other conditions. Laennec taught the art of auscultation and profoundly changed the way medicine was practiced. How many lives did Laennec save with his invention? How much human misery was avoided by his discovery? It is hard to imagine the potential ignominy of withholding of this invention for family gain.

Professor Ian Donald, a more recent example of inventive genius, made an enormous impact on the practice of medicine by an invention. Donald, born in 1910 in Cornwall, was the son of a general practitioner who lived in Scotland and South Africa where his father practiced medicine. He received his medical degree from the University of London and eventually was appointed to the Regius Chair of Midwifery at Glasgow in 1954. Together with a brilliant engineer, Tom Brown, they employed some sonar equipment that was used to detect German submarines during World War II, to craft the first compound sonogram scanner. Although rudimentary compared to current 3-D and 4-D scanners, it was capable of 3-D imaging of the fetus, and marked the beginning of the field of medical sonography. Ian Donald's instrument worked by beaming harmless sound waves into the uterus, which reflected off the fetus and bounced back, providing an image on a screen. This highly respected academic physician has been referred to as the *Father of Sonography*. There is a classic picture of Ian Donald scanning his pregnant daughter's uterus, thus showing three generations simultaneously. Professor Ian Donald continued to develop the technique and, of course, industry immediately became involved in developing real-time ultrasound and a myriad of improvements since Donald's prototype. This modality has enabled detection of early pregnancy, determining fetal age and size, surveys of fetal anatomy, and enabled diagnostic and therapeutic procedures to name but a few. It has been extremely valuable in gynecology in detecting and monitoring fibroids in the uterus, ovarian cysts, detecting cancer, and a huge list of other practical indications. If asked what the three greatest contributions to obstetrics and gynecology have been in the last four decades, I would reply ultrasound, ultrasound, and ultrasound. This invention has been responsible for saving countless lives. Indeed, had Professor Donald not invented this modality or had he kept it a family secret, can you imagine what would have happened over these last decades to the welfare of mothers and babies?

It was not until the beginning of the eighteenth century that the secret of the Chamberlens' became well known. In 1733 Edmund Chapman, a country surgeon and midwife in the nearby Essex area published a scientific discourse on the forceps, entitled *"A Treatise on the Improvement of Midwifery."* He indicated that several versions of forceps had been available for some time. He gave credit to the Chamberlens for the original invention. No other instruments had been in evidence in England or on the Continent up to this time.

This means that from the time of hiding the forceps after Peter's death in 1683 until Chapman's report, there were three to four decades when the forceps, a highly significant medical discovery, was not available to effect improvement in the practice of midwifery. A more critical view is that from the discovery in approximately 1595 until around 1725, some 130 years, the impact of a significant medical discovery, the first opportunity in the history of midwifery to intervene safely in the course of a problem labor, was withheld from its natural influence to improve the practice of childbirth.

Chapman was the first to mention the forceps in print and gave an illustration of the Gifford's forceps, first used by Gifford on April 20, 1726, and referred to as *an extractor* and was in use locally. Of note, Chapman kept secret his method of delivery with the fillet, concerning which he said, "I must beg to leave to be silent as being an Invention of my own: nor shall I, I hope be censured for my doing so, any more than the great Dr. Chamberlen was for his choosing to conceal the method or secret whereby he could extract children without hooks where other artists were forced to use them" (Speert 2004). As a reminder of the primitive level of medicine being practiced at the time, Chapman writes that when a patient has had a hard labor there is nothing so good as to cover the body with sheepskin "hastily flead off and applied as warm as possible."

What effect would have the timely promulgation of the forceps had on midwifery practice? The forceps could have provided the force of change. For starters, the forceps would have decreased the infant and maternal deaths in many prolonged labors. In the words of Peter Chamberlen "The benefits being computed (over and above the bettering of health and strength to Parents and Children) to the saving of above three thousand lives a year in and about London, beside the rest of England, and all other parts where the same Order might have been propagated" (Aveling 1882, page 50). The number of newborn injuries due to birth trauma could have been reduced. The introduction of forceps would have accelerated the entry of barber-surgeons into the practice of childbirth. The immediate effect of this would have increased the involvement of individuals with education, training, and standards into the practice of midwifery. Of course, it is highly speculative, but had the Chamberlens freely given the secret to society, most likely they would not have met such fierce opposition to their proposal for teaching and incorporation of midwives in London.

By far the biggest benefit would have been the impetus for change in requirements for education and training because the forceps offered the first safe intervention in prolonged labors. The barber-surgeons might have had more involvement in childbirth, and the training and education of midwives might have been given higher status than that provided by the Church of England.

By the 1700's the lying-in movement had begun in England with hospitals dedicated to childbirth springing up throughout the country. The promulgation of the forceps could have catalyzed this movement a century earlier, perhaps even making England the world leader in midwifery.

Certainly there was progress in the 17th Century England, as evidenced by the involvement of more literate midwives, for by 1660 most could read and write. There was additional advancement when Madames Shaw and Whipp opposed the Chamberlens from incorporating the midwives because they were challenged to show what they could do for education and standards that was better than what the Chamberlens were offering. Finally, talented midwives such as Jane Sharp, Miss Willughby, and Elizabeth Collier made much progress when they appeared on the birthing scene.

Had the forceps been available to the world in say 1600, certain practices would have evolved. Whereas the midwives would have continued to perform most of the deliveries, the barber surgeons would have been more involved in problem deliveries. The Barber Surgeons Company certainly would have systematized education and practice, just as the College of Physicians would have for the midwives if the Archbishops had allowed it, when offered in 1634. The Chamberlens' attempts to incorporate the midwives were the impetus for the midwives to form their own guild. Sadly they did not gain recognition until 1902, almost three centuries later, when they were granted independent status in England. For a profession that has been in existence from early history they were unfortunately held back by many factors, few of which were their own doing. Fortunately today modern midwifery in England is characterized by excellent education, training, certification, standards and exemplary practice.

Chapter 54   How Has Obstetrics Evolved?

Childbirth has changed remarkably over time. Having concentrated on childbirth as it was three centuries ago in this historical biography, I would now like to bring us up to date. Since our story focused on childbirth in England, I will compare contemporary childbirth in England with that in the United States. Although in both countries most babies are born by normal spontaneous deliveries, England and the United States have very different systems for childbirth.

England has a system of approximately 28,000 midwives providing prenatal care to most pregnant women and delivering their children through the National Health System. Physicians become involved when there are complications and when operative deliveries using forceps, vacuum extractions, or cesareans are performed. Some physicians also provide primary obstetrical care to women with high-risk pregnancies. In addition, some have private obstetrical practices, but in England they are in the minority.

The United States has a system of approximately 50,000 physicians who provide prenatal care and both spontaneous and operative deliveries. Nurse midwives provide prenatal care and deliver approximately 11% of uncomplicated, spontaneous childbirths.

In England midwives typically complete a three to four year degree course that leads to certification by the Nursing and Midwifery Council. The education is usually split equally between coursework at a university and hands-on clinical practice. Physicians typically have a six year college course ending with a Bachelor of Medicine before they train for four more years in Obstetrics and Gynecology to be eligible for written and oral exams for certification by the Royal College of Obstetricians and Gynaecologists. Most of the health professionals are employed by the National Health Service.

In the United States nurse midwives are generally graduates of degree nursing programs who then train for 18-24 months in midwifery, often receiving a Master's degree. Midwives may be employed by hospitals or physician groups, or practice in midwifery groups. Physicians typically complete four years of college for a degree, then four years of medical school for a Doctor of Medicine followed by four more years of specialty training in Obstetrics and Gynecology. They take written board exams, and if successful, after a year of practice, take the oral board exam of the American Board of Obstetrics and Gynecology. Physicians generally join a group practice, or are employed by hospitals or insurance organizations. The concept of solo practice is rapidly declining in the United States.

In both countries, the education and training are long and rigorous, assuring the public of highly educated and skilled health professionals. Throughout history midwifery has been a women's profession and obstetrics a men's profession. In recent decades, however, the number of women entering Obstetrics and Gynecology has increased considerably so that women are quickly becoming the majority.

The mode of delivery has also changed remarkably over time. In the Chamberlen era all deliveries were through the vagina. Forceps were the first solution for treating prolonged labor and they remained so for centuries. After Chapman published his treatise on forceps in 1733, these instruments were used by "man midwives" in England and on the Continent to deliver babies for mothers whose labors were prolonged by numerous factors: large babies, a difficult position of the baby, or maternal exhaustion. Of course, there were no cesarean deliveries at this time, so forceps were extremely valuable additions to midwifery.

In the 1950s Dr. Malmström introduced the metal cup vacuum extractor and it promptly became an alternative to the forceps. The soft cup vacuum extractors and hand-held vacuum pumps, introduced in the 1980s made the use of vacuum extractors more popular. Both vacuum extractors and forceps were used to avoid the risks of major surgery associated with cesarean deliveries and are acceptable and safe instruments for operative vaginal deliveries. In the 1990s, approximately 9% of deliveries were operative vaginal, declining to 5% in the last decade. In the last two decades vacuum extractors were used progressively more commonly than forceps. The decreased use of forceps has created a dilemma. There are fewer skilled operators who can teach physicians in-training this technique, which will further decrease their use in the future.

In the 20th century, cesarean deliveries changed considerably as they became safer with the advent of good anesthesia, blood transfusions, and antibiotics. Cesareans are performed for failure to progress in labor, multiple pregnancies when the presenting baby is breech, concern for the baby's well-being (as with abnormal fetal heart beat patterns), problems with the placenta, and even for maternal request.

Although cesareans are now quite safe and hospital stays are as short as two or three days, cesareans entail major surgery as the mother's abdomen and uterus are entered during the operation.

Today the numerous options available to the obstetrician for operative deliveries facilitate the possibility of decreasing mortality and morbidity. Operative deliveries can be life-saving and prevent compromise to the baby, but they also have the possibility of causing injury. A study of 83,340 singleton deliveries from 1992-1994 in California provided information concerning risk of injury. As one would expect, the lowest risk of fetal injury was found in spontaneous vaginal deliveries. An intermediate risk was found in those deliveries by vacuum extractor or forceps alone or by cesarean delivery during labor. The highest risk of injury was reported in infants delivered by combined forceps and vacuum, or who were delivered by cesarean after failed operative vaginal delivery (Towner 1999).

The use of cesareans has grown exponentially. In the 1960s the cesarean section rate was 5.5%, but today the frequency of this mode of delivery has reached 33%. When patients have cesarean deliveries, commonly their future deliveries are by cesareans. Even though vaginal birth after cesarean has been shown to be safe in appropriate patients, it has not been a popular choice. It is reasonable to estimate that the cesarean rate will continue rise. Options for delivery are far greater than those available to the Chamberlens. Today, one third of the deliveries are through the abdominal wall. The Chamberlens never had the luxury of that option.

Chapter 55   Visit to Maldon

I was so intrigued with the mystery of the forceps that I felt compelled to see first-hand where they were hidden for over a century. That scene was clearly Maldon, the site of the last three decades of Peter Chamberlen's life. I was determined to visit Woodham Mortimer Hall to see for myself. After googling Maldon I saw that Woodham Mortimer Hall was now a registered historic landmark. The Chamber of Commerce told me I could visit the manor house by appointment. I excitedly phoned the owners. Mrs. Janet Doe answered and told me she would be very happy to show me the house at an agreed upon time. Of course, with a name like Janet Doe I wanted some sort of reality check for "John and Jane Doe" are the fictitious names we encounter daily in the US for hypothetical, often untrue situations. In a charming manner she assured me that this was truly her name and that my wife Carrie and I would be welcomed guests at Woodham Mortimer Hall.

Landing at Heathrow, we drove to Cambridge to visit the site of Dr. Peter's education. We did make a misjudgment when the airport Hertz agent told us they were having a special on car rentals; a Mercedes was available for just a few pounds more per day than the practical car I had reserved. Well it was new, shiny, large, and it drove like a dream on the motorways. But Maldon and surrounding areas are crisscrossed by narrow roads, high hedgerows and, of course, England had a different orientation on which side of the road to travel. I must confess en route we had some harrowing near-misses.

At the outskirts of Maldon, on our way down from Cambridge, we encountered an earth-colored mountain on the right side of the road. It was an enormous pile of potatoes deposited on the roadside waiting to be trucked away. Good evidence of the fertile farmlands of East Anglia that had made Maldon an important port of call. We were getting close. I could tell. Proceeding along the London Road, an apparition suddenly loomed on the left. Unmistakably, it was Woodham Mortimer Hall, with its three dormers and prominent chimneys. Even with the "new" brick wall obscuring the front garden and the first floor, I knew this was it. I immediately pulled off the road to gape at this home, stately, proud, and holding many of the secrets. But I would have to wait for our appointment was not until the next morning.

We made our way into Maldon, across the Blackwater River and headed north to find the 16th century farmhouse we had booked bed and breakfast. The skies darkened, down came torrents of rain, causing me to slow and ultimately stop. Then just as quickly, the rain ceased, out came the sun and a rainbow arced in the west. I have always believed in good omens and this was clearly a favorable sign.

The farmhouse was charming as was the couple who ran the bed and breakfast. Of course, they knew Colin and Janet Doe. I was growing more excited every minute and was anxious to set off in the morning for the visit. Following a hearty breakfast including a rasher of bacon produced on the farm we bid goodbye and set out.

On arrival at Woodham Mortimer Hall, the gate swung open electronically, and Mrs. Janet Doe was at the door to greet us. Our tour of the house revealed an entry room with a line-up of carefully arranged wellies. The grand rooms with high ceilings all had fireplaces. The house was in excellent condition and reminded me of what 16-17th century living must have been like. Then Janet said, "I am sure you want to see the hiding place. My son is at college and he uses the dormer as a closet. I have removed all of his things so you can see the trap door."

Up the stairs we went, camera in hand, in great anticipation. There it was in the floor, just as it was over three centuries ago, a trap door with sunken hinges. Janet lifted the lid and we peered into medical history, or perhaps I should say medical mystery. It wasn't the trap door and it wasn't the hiding place: it was the choice to keep this valuable invention a secret for well over a century that was the compelling historic mystery.

The Trap Door

Then all went downstairs and out the garden door led by Janet's West Highland Terrier. We turned left for 10 paces, no more, and we were at the gate to the St. Margaret's churchyard where Dr. Chamberlen was entombed. Janet unlocked the gate and there, right in front of me was the memorial erected by his son, Hope Chamberlen, with the inscriptions and the poem by Dr. Peter Chamberlen, composed for the occasion of his death.

251

After reading a sea of books on the subject, in one morning I was actually seeing the sites where so much took place. The reality of the scene was a powerful incentive to learn more. At that juncture Janet showed us to a room where she had laid on a long table some 28 references on the Chamberlens. I had seen probably 17 or18 of these. The remaining ones were very helpful, mainly informative local articles concerning the history of Woodham Mortimer Hall. Carrie and I were extremely indebted to Janet Doe for a most valuable visit, one that she wedged in before departing with her daughter for an admission interview at university. At Woodham Mortimer Hall, thanks to Janet Doe, we had gained vivid and vital information and were getting closer to understanding the mystery.

In 1683, at age 82, Dr. Chamberlen died quietly at Woodham Mortimer Hall. Thirteen decades later, in June of 1813 Mrs. Kemball was visiting her grandchildren who resided in Woodham Mortimer Hall. She discovered the secret hiding place that contained the treasure trove of medical instruments and memorabilia. Initially bewildered by what was discovered, she and her son-in-law, Mr. Codd, sought help from a friend, Mr. Henry Carwardine, a surgeon. Mr. Carwardine had retired to Earls Colne, a village 10 miles north of Maldon, a few years before and was writing a book on the history of surgery. Mr. Codd thought that with his knowledge of medical history and surgery Mr. Carwardine perhaps could help unravel the mystery of these items (Aveling 1882).

As a historian, Mr. Carwardine knew about the Chamberlens and their secret instruments. Indeed, in 1733, some 50 years after Dr. Peter Chamberlen died, Dr. Chapman, a country surgeon practicing in Essex, had published a midwifery text which described obstetrical forceps and their use in childbirth. Soon thereafter the use of forceps became widespread in the urban areas of Europe.

When Mr. Carwardine saw the instruments, he became very excited. He knew what obstetrical forceps looked like and how they were used, so it was easy for him to recognize the significance of this finding. The old Bible found with the cache of instruments, with its inscription, seemed to establish ownership by Dr. Chamberlen.

Cache of Obstetrical Instruments Hidden Below the Floorboards (Courtesy of the Royal College of Obstetricians and Gynaecologists)

Over the next two days, Mr. Codd and Mr. Carwardine recorded the precise description and measurements of the instruments. The Codds believed the instruments should be donated to a medical museum in order to promulgate the

253

importance of the discovery. At the request of the Codds, Mr. Carwardine contacted the directors of the Medical and Chirurgical Society of London to enquire if they were interested. An immediate reply from the directors indicated they would most gratefully receive the instruments for the Society museum.

In 1690 Hugh developed a land bank scheme fashioned on the Amsterdam system that ended in financial disaster, forcing him to flee to Holland, where ironically he died in poverty. The competing bank scheme that survived is today the Bank of England. Some say Hugh tried to sell the secret instrument in Holland. Whether that actually occurred is difficult to document; however, the nature of the man leaves little doubt that he probably did so. In 1702, he published a scheme for the Union of Scotland and England, entitled "The Great Advantages to Both Kingdoms of Scotland and England by a Union – by a Friend to Britain, 1702. Aveling wrote: "It is very remarkable that this, the last of all the projects proposed by the Chamberlens should have been the only one destined to be realized."

The invention and the use of the secret instrument by the Chamberlen family catalyzed the entry of male barber-surgeons into the exclusively female domain of assisting the birthing process. The Chamberlens' attempt to organize the London midwives provided the impetus for midwives to form their own guild, although they did not gain official recognition until 1902, almost three centuries later.

The invention of the forceps enabled trained men to enter the all-female world of childbirth, motivated improvement in midwifery, and saved many lives. The development of this innovative medical device was driven by passion to improve the birth process but tainted by a desire for personal wealth. How many lives were saved by the forceps? How many lives were lost by not revealing the secret? How much was medical progress retarded by not revealing this important discovery?

Epilogue

Today the original secret forceps reside in the Royal College of Obstetricians and Gynaecologists, 27 Sussex Place, Regent's Park, London, symbolizing inventive genius and a family secret.

THE END

Discoveries, Approximate Year

Obstetrical forceps - 1595
Stethoscope - 1816
Cause of childbed fever (Semmelweiss) - 1847
Blood transfusion - 1854
Lister's antiseptic technique - 1867
Cesarean delivery (greater than 50% mortality) - 1878
Roentgenogram – 1895
Blood Banking - 1940
Penicillin - 1944
Sonography - 1950
Safe Cesarean delivery - 1950 onwards

Bibliography

Ackroyd, Peter. 2000. *London: the biography*. New York: Nan A. Talese.

Aslet, Clive. 1999. *The story of Greenwich*. Cambridge, Mass: Harvard University Press.

Aveling, J. H. 1882. *The Chamberlens and the midwifery forceps: memorials of the family, and an essay on the invention of the instrument*. London: J. & A. Churchill.

Aveling, James Hobson. 1872. *English Midwives: their history and prospects*. J. & J. Churchill: London.

Baskett, T. E. 1997. "Operative Vaginal Delivery in the 21st Century". *JOURNAL- SOGC*. 19 (4): 355-357.

Birch, Thomas. 1848. *The court and times of Charles the First*. London: H. Colburn.

Burton, Elizabeth. 1962. *The Jacobeans at home*. London: Secker & Warburg.

Cellier, Elizabeth. *The Mid-wives just petition, or, A complaint of divers good gentlewomen of that faculty shewing to the whole Christian world their just cause of their sufferings in these distracted times, for their want of trading : vvhich said complaint they tendered to the House on Monday last, being the 23 of Ian. 1643 : with some other notes worthy of observation*. 1643. Printed at London: [s.n.].

Chailly-Honoré, Nicolas Charles. 1864. *Tratado práctico del arte de partear*. Madrid: Impr. de Gaspar y Roig.

Chamberlen, Peter. 1647. *A voice in Rhama or, The crie of women and children. Ecchoed forth in the compassions of Peter*

Chamberlen, Doctour in Physick, Fellow of the Colledge of London, and one of his Majesties physicians extraordinary. London: Printed by William Bentley: for John Marshall, and are to be sold at his shop at the Hand and Pen in Corn-hill, over against the Royall Exchange.

Cook, Judith. 2001. *Dr Simon Forman: a most notorious physician.* London: Chatto & Windus.

Dobyns, Kenneth. *Patent Office History.* http://myoutbox.net/pohome.htm. (December 4, 2012).

Donnison, Jean. 1977. *Midwives and medical men: a history of inter-professional rivalries and women's rights.* New York: Schocken Books.

Dunn PM. 1999. "The Chamberlen family (1560-1728) and obstetric forceps". *Archives of Disease in Childhood. Fetal and Neonatal Edition.* 81 (3): 232-4.

Encyclopedia Britannica. 2002. *Encyclopedia britannica.* Chicago, IL: Encyclopedia Britannica.

Evenden, Doreen. 2000. *The midwives of seventeenth-century London.* Cambridge [England]: Cambridge University Press.

Goodall, Charles. 1684. *The Royal College of Physicians of London, founded and established by law as appears by letters patents, acts of Parliament, adjudged cases, &c. And An historical account of the College's proceedings against empiricks and unlicensed practisers in every princes reign from their first incorporation to the murther of the royal martyr, King Charles the First.* London: Printed by M. Flesher for W. Kettilby.

Graham, Harvey. 1960. *Eternal Eve. The mysteries of birth and the customs that surround it. (Revised edition.).* London: Hutchinson.

Loggan, David. 1675. *Cantabrigia illustrata sive omnium celeberrimae istius universitatis collegiorum, aularum, bibliothecae academicae, scholarum publicarum sacelli coll. regales nec non totius oppidi ichnographia.*

MacDonald C. 1952. "Religio medici". *The Medical Journal of Australia.* 2 (15).

Mauriceau, François. 1752. *The diseases of women with child, and in child-bed as also, the best means of helping them in natural and unnatural labours. ... To which is prefix'd, an exact description of the parts of generation in women. ... The eighth edition corrected, and augmented with several new figures ... Written in French by Francis Mauriceau, and translated by Hugh Chamberlen, M.D.* London: Printed for T. Cox, and J. Clarke.

Pepys, Samuel, Robert Latham, and William Matthews. 1970. *The diary of Samuel Pepys.* Berkeley: University of California Press.

Radcliffe, Walter, and Walter Radcliffe. 1989. *Milestones in midwifery ; and, The secret instrument (The birth of the midwifery forceps).* San Francisco: Norman Pub.

Royal College of Medicine. *Roll of Students.* Ledger. Not published. Royal College of Medicine, *Collection name with dates.* (Accessed June 4 2003).

Sawyer, Edmund, and Ralph Winwood. 1972. *Memorials of affairs of state in the reigns of Q. Elizabeth and K. James I. 2. (1972). - 492 S.* London: Ward.

Shaw, Hester. 1653. *Mrs. Shaws innocency restored, and Mr. Clendons calumny retorted notwithstanding his late triumphing. By sundry depositions, making out more than ever she by discourse or writing did positively charge upon him.* 1653. London.

Smellie, William, Petrus Camper, Jan van Rymsdyk, and Charles Grignion. 1754. *A sett of anatomical tables, with explanations, and an abridgment, of the practice of midwifery, with a view to illustrate a treatise on that subject, and collection of cases.* London.

Speert, Harold. 2004. *Obstetrics and gynecology: a history and iconography.* New York: Parthenon Pub. Group.

Towler, Jean, and Joan Bramall. 1986. *Midwives in history and society.* London: Croom Helm.

Towner, D, Castro MA, Eby-Wilkens E, Gilbert EM. Effect of mode of delivery in nulliparous women on neonatal intracranial injury. N Engl J Med 1999; 341: 1709-1714.

Trueman, Chris. *History Learning Site.* http://www.historylearningsite.co.uk/ (December 4, 2012).

Charles, James, William, Mary, and Joseph Williamson. 1992. *The complete state papers domestic, 1509-1702 Unit 32, Series II, Part 22, Reel 477. Unit 33, Series II, Part 23, Reels 499-521. Unit 34, Series II, Part 24, Reels 522-541.* Woodbridge, CT: Thomson Gale Primary Source Microfilm.

Willughby, Percival, and Henry Blenkinsop. 1972. *Observations in midwifery.* Wakefield: S.R. Publishers.

Wilson, Adrian. 1995. *The making of man-midwifery: childbirth in England, 1660-1770.* Cambridge, Mass: Harvard University Press.

Winwood, Ralph, and Edmund Sawyer. 1725. *Memorials of affairs of state in the reigns of queen Elizabeth and king James I: collected , chiefly from the original papers of Ralph Winwood : comprehending likewise the Negotiations of Hen. Neville ... at the Corts of France and Spain, and in Holland, Venice.*

For Book Club Readers

1. How did the forceps save lives in the 17th century?

2. How do midwives of the 17th century compare to present day midwives?

3. Should the Church of England have accepted the offer of the College of Physicians to vet new midwives in the 17th century?

4. How does the education of modern physicians differ from the 17th century?

5. Describe the relationship of a member of court to the King or Queen

6. How do patents during the reigns of Queen Elizabeth and King James1 compare to modern day patents

7. Is the addition of the author's recreations of scenes helpful to the reader? Is there a better approach?

If you wish to send comments, they would be welcome: jtqmd@aol.com

John Thomas Queenan, M.D. is a graduate of the University of Notre Dame and Weill Cornell University School of Medicine. His graduate education was at Bellevue Hospital and the New York Hospital Cornell Medical Center where he trained in obstetrics and gynecology. Dr. Queenan spent his career in academic medicine with a love for patients and clinical research, pioneering work in sonography, international public health, and diagnosis and treatment of the fetus. He was an Associate Professor of Obstetrics and Gynecology at Cornell, and Professor and Chair of Obstetrics and Gynecology at University of Louisville School of Medicine, and Georgetown University School of Medicine. It was during his two London sabbaticals that he became fascinated with the mystery of the Chamberlens' forceps. As founder and editor of Contemporary OB/GYN for 28 years, he had an enormous influence in medical education. The former Deputy Editor of Obstetrics & Gynecology, he has written more than 160 scientific papers and 21 textbooks. The recipient of many honors and awards, his most valued is the establishment of the Queenan Fellowships in Global Health by The Society for Maternal Fetal Medicine and The Pregnancy Foundation. Dr. Queenan loves to ski, play tennis, and paint in oils, but is content going on adventures and just hanging out with his wife, Carrie.

Made in the USA
San Bernardino, CA
01 June 2015